MW00423622

1 — SELF CONTROL · GOODNESS · TRUTH · PERFECTION · CLARITY · JUSTICE ·

2 — HELPFULNESS · ALTRUISM · LOVING · BOLD · SERVANTS HEART · DISCERNING NEEDS ·

3 — EFFICIENCY · ACTION · ENCOURAGER · ESTABLISHER · INSPIRING · EXCELLENCE ·

4 — CREATIVITY · EMPATHY · LOVE OF BEAUTY · SPACE SAVER · EMOTIONALLY HONEST ·

5 — WISDOM · VISION · STEADFASTNESS · CLARITY · FAITHFULNESS · HUMILITY ·

6 — COURAGE · GUARDIANSHIP · KINDNESS · LOYALTY · STRENGTH · FAITHFULNESS ·

7 — SPONTANEITY · JOY · THANKFULNESS · HOPE · LONG SUFFERING · VISION ·

8 — STRENGTH · ZEAL · VIGILANT · JUSTICE · PROTECTOR · TENDERNESS ·

9 — PEACE · KINDNESS · EMPATHY · PATIENCE · GENTLENESS · UNDERSTANDING ·

WHAT PEOPLE ARE SAYING ABOUT ELISABETH BENNETT AND *THE PERFECTIONIST: GROWING AS AN ENNEAGRAM 1*

With nuance and kindness, Elisabeth offers Ones, myself included, a steady, gentle path to self-awareness. I love how she dismantles the stereotype of Ones while simultaneously showing great compassion for the essence of who we are. I'm grateful these words exist.

—*Kendra Adachi*
Podcaster and author, *The Lazy Genius Way*

Elisabeth has written a delightful devotional full of important information for those who want to grow in their own self-awareness and relationship with Christ. I highly recommend reading this book so you can experience transformation on a much deeper level that will bring about the change you desire in life.

—*Beth McCord*
YourEnneagramCoach.com
Author of 10 Enneagram books

Elisabeth has a beautiful way of guiding the reader into a deeper understanding and self-awareness that leads to spiritual growth through the Enneagram. Through biblically sound and practical devotions, she helps you move from, "Okay, I know what type I am but what's next?" to personal, relational, and spiritual growth, so that you can live in the fullness of who you were created to be in your unique type.

—*Justin Boggs*
The Other Half Podcast
Enneagram coach, speaker, entrepreneur

Through her beautifully articulate words, Elisabeth accurately portrays the shadow side of each Enneagram type while also highlighting the rich grace and freedom found in the spiritual journey of integration. Pairing Scripture with reflection questions and prayers, the devotions help guide the reader on the pathway of personal and spiritual growth in a powerful way that is unique to their type.

—*Meredith Boggs*
The Other Half Podcast

If you know your Enneagram type and you're ready to make meaningful steps toward growth, this book is for you. Elisabeth combines her Enneagram expertise with her deep faith to guide readers toward self-understanding, growth, and transformation through contemplative yet practical writing. This devotional is a great tool that you'll return to again and again.

—*Steph Barron Hall*
Nine Types Co.

60-DAY
ENNEAGRAM DEVOTIONAL

the
PERFECTIONIST

GROWING AS AN ENNEAGRAM

ELISABETH BENNETT

WHITAKER
HOUSE

Introduction images created by Katherine Waddell.
Photo of Elisabeth Bennett by Jena Stagner of One Beautiful Life Photography.

The Perfectionist
Growing as an Enneagram 1

www.elisabethbennettenneagram.com
Instagram: @enneagram.life
Facebook.com/enneagramlife

ISBN: 978-1-64123-568-6 • eBook ISBN: 978-1-64123-569-3
Printed in the United States of America
© 2021 by Elisabeth Bennett

Whitaker House
1030 Hunt Valley Circle
New Kensington, PA 15068
www.whitakerhouse.com

Library of Congress Cataloging-in-Publication Data (Pending)

1 2 3 4 5 6 7 8 9 10 11 � 28 27 26 25 24 23 22 21

DEDICATION

To all the Ones holding this devotional, you're good,
righteous, and perfected in Christ.

Contents

FOREWORD

I feel like I'm sitting in a room of people who *get me* right now. We could all swap stories of how our husbands load the dishwasher wrong (bless his heart), how unorganized our children are, or how our bosses just don't get us. You would all laugh—not *at* me, because you do it too!—when I tell you the story about how I have an itemized list of our family vacation and I would nod in agreement when you share about how you are going to single-handedly fix all of the world's injustice.

Who runs the world? *ONES.*

After I found out I was a One, I was a little resentful about it for a while. Why couldn't I be fun like a Seven or ambitious like a Four? I don't want to be the boring One! Then I started learning more about me and the wonderful things I bring to my family, my church, and my community as a One. And I wouldn't have it any other way!

When I was a teenager, I discovered Matthew 5:48: *"You therefore must be perfect, as your heavenly Father is perfect."* I'm pretty sure I jumped up and did a little dance the first time I read that. I was so thrilled because right there in the Bible was my out! If Scripture is telling me to strive to be perfect, then it must be right! I spent so much of my life attempting to be perfect. The perfect wife. The perfect mom. The perfect leader. The perfect writer.

But here's the deal: I took it completely out of context. (Shocking, I know.) As a One, when we hear the word *perfect*, it

9

becomes a comfort for us. Perfection is always what we are working toward, and I have found this becomes intensified for Ones who are Christ followers.

For the sake of authenticity and lack of perfection, I have to confess, I spent entirely too much time overthinking this foreword. Isn't that how it goes, my fellow Ones? We wouldn't dare miss a deadline, but we will work ourselves to the bone to make sure something is perfect. (Or procrastinate because we're afraid it won't be good enough! My Nine wing gets me there!) I'm going to do my best to put aside worrying about making sure I write the perfect few pages.

I don't want to bring you perfection today, but a promise.

I want to assure you that your hard work and your dedication to details is all worth it—but that won't bring you fulfillment at the end of the day. I don't have to tell you twice; as a One, nothing will ever be good enough for us. We can continue to make changes to our work, our relationships, and even ourselves but always find a mistake. This is where we have to realize that *only Christ is without flaw.*

Let's go back to the word *perfect* we see in this Scripture I mentioned. When I realized that this verse wasn't a comfort for *everyone*, I thought maybe I was looking at it all wrong. The Greek word for perfect used here is *teleios*, which means maturity, wholeness, or complete. Maybe perfect isn't the best translation, especially for Ones like us. The goal isn't perfection, but to be complete like our Father as we continue to mirror Him. Our calling as Christians isn't to perfection, and we can allow God to be even more glorified through our imperfection.

I'm honored to welcome you into the next sixty days. I encourage you to be willing to put aside the rules a bit—I know it's hard!—and ask God to root out any ugliness from your heart. We Ones tend to hang on to anger and bitterness. We play judge and jury. It's time to set those natural tendencies aside because God wants to do this work in you. And I promise the work will be worth it.

—*Kara-Kae James*
Author, *Mom Up: Thriving with Grace in the Chaos of Motherhood*
Host, *Asking for a Friend* Podcast

ACKNOWLEDGMENTS

My journey from young hopeful writer, all the way back to the tender age of four, to holding books with my name on them hasn't been easy or pretty. In fact, it's held a lot of hurt, disappointment, and rejection. However, as you hold a book with my name on the cover in your hands, I'd love you to know who and what has sustained me through it all. You are holding a piece of God's redemption in my story, tangible proof of His kindness, and testament of His faithfulness. I didn't break any doors down or *do* anything myself that ensured my trajectory of publishing. God in His kindness handed me this opportunity, and to Him alone belongs all the glory and praise.

My agent Amanda deserves the highest of thanks and admiration. Thank you for answering my many questions, guiding, and giving me the confidence to do this. I couldn't have done it without you. To all the people at Whitaker House, my editor Peg and publisher Christine, thank you for making these devotionals what they are today. It's been a pleasure working with you all.

To my writing community hope*writers, thank you for giving me the courage to call myself a writer long before I felt like one. To Kara-Kae James, thank you for being one of the first pair of eyes on this devotional and for writing such an encouraging foreword! Your words and your heart for your fellow Ones are so beautiful. Thank you to Pastor Bubba Jennings at Resurrection Church for reading over my proposal and giving me advice on how to serve Jesus well in this process.

The people who have been the biggest support and help to me during this process, and if I'm honest, my life, are:

Lydia Sergio, thank you so much for being a part of this project! I'm so grateful for the time, effort, and months you put into making this devotional a tangible reflection of your heart for your fellow Ones. Thank you!

To all the other Ones in my life who have left a big impact on my heart, as well as my ability to write this devotional: Peter Bennett, Hadassah Bennett, Lydia Sergio, Tammy Thomas Rohrbaugh, John A. Bennett, Kendra Adachi, all my Enneagram One clients, and a couple other suspected Ones whom I won't publicly *type* here. Thank you!

Sarah Upton, thank you for faithfully helping with Wellington during this entire journey. I am so comfortable when he is with you, and I adore how much you love him.

Mikayla Larson, thank you for your friendship, support, and for being here when I've needed you the most. You are such a gift in my life.

John and Jan Bennett, thank you for faithfully praying for me and supporting me through this entire process. Your encouragement has moved mountains and sustained me on the hardest days.

Thank you, Mom and Dad (Joe and Diane Upton), for literally teaching me to read and write and encouraging me to say yes to big things. I would never have had the foundation to say yes without you and how you raised me. I'm so proud and grateful to have the two of you in my corner cheering me on.

Peter, you've been beyond supporting, patient, and caring toward me. I don't know what else I would've expected from a One. You have taught me so much about what it means to be faithful, and you never let me quit. You believe in me enough for both of us, and I can't believe the gift that you are in my life. Thank you for helping me with this devotional in particular, and for giving me so many real-life examples to work with. You're my best friend and I love you.

INTRODUCTION
What Is the Enneagram?

The Enneagram is an ancient personality typology for which no one really knows the origins.

It uses nine points within a circle—the word itself means "a drawing of nine"—to represent nine distinct personality types. The points are numbered simply to differentiate between them, with each point having no greater or less value than the others. The theory is that a person assumes one of these personalities in childhood as a reaction to discovering that the world is a scary, unkind place that is unlikely to accept their true self.

The nine types are identified by their numbers or by these names:

1. The Perfectionist
2. The Helper
3. The Achiever
4. The Individualist
5. The Thinker
6. The Guardian
7. The Enthusiast
8. The Challenger
9. The Peacemaker

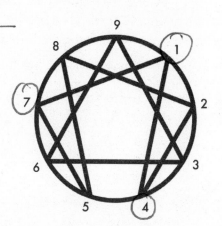

HOW DO I FIND MY TYPE?

Your Enneagram type is determined by your main motivation. Finding your Enneagram type is a journey, as we are typically unaware of our motivations and instead focus on our behaviors. Many online tests focus on behaviors, and while some motivations *may* produce certain behaviors, this may not always be the case, and you are unlikely to get accurate results.

To find your Enneagram type, you need to start by learning about *all* nine Enneagram types and explore their motivations in contrast to your own behaviors and deeper motivations.

You can ask for feedback from those around you, but most often, the more you learn, the clearer your core number shines through.

It's often the number whose description makes you feel the most *exposed* that is your true core type. Your core Enneagram number won't change, since it's solidified in childhood.

Each number's distinct motivation:

1. <u>Integrity – Goodness</u>
2. Love – Relationships
3. Worth – Self-Importance
4. Authenticity – Unique Identity
5. Competency – Objective Truth
6. Security – Guidance
7. Satisfaction – Freedom
8. Independence – Control
9. Peace – Equilibrium

IS THIS JOURNEY WORTH IT?

Yes! The self-awareness you gain along the way is gold, and learning about the other types in the process brings you so much empathy and understanding for all of the other personalities in your life.

WHAT MAKES THE ENNEAGRAM UNIQUE AND DIFFERENT FROM MYERS-BRIGGS, STRENGTHSFINDER, OR DISC ASSESSMENTS?

The Enneagram, unlike other typology systems, is fluid. Yes, the Enneagram tells you what your base personality characteristics are, but it also reveals how you change when you're growing, stressed, secure, unhealthy, healthy, etc.

You are not the same person at twenty as you are at sixty. You're not the same person at your stressful workplace as you are when binge-watching your favorite TV show and eating ice cream at home. The Enneagram accounts for these inconsistencies and changes in your behavior and informs you of when or how those changes occur.

If you look at the following graph, you'll see that each of the numbers connects to two other numbers by arrows. The arrow pointed toward your number is your growth arrow; the arrow pointed away is your stress number. When your life leaves you with more room to breathe, you exhibit positive characteristics of your growth number, and when you're stretched thin in seasons of stress, you exhibit the negative characteristics of your stress number.

This is one explanation for big shifts in personality over a lifetime.

Another point of difference between the Enneagram and other typology systems is *wings*. Your wings are the two numbers on either side of your core number, which add flavor to your personality type. Although your core number won't change—and your main motivation, sin proclivities, and personality will come from that core number—your wings can be very influential on your overall personality and how it presents itself. There are many different theories about wings, but the viewpoint we hold to is:

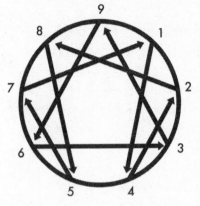

+ Your wing can only be one of the two numbers on either side of your number. Therefore, you can be a 1 with a 2 wing (1w2) but not a 1 with an 8 wing (1w8).

+ You have access to the numbers on either side of your number, but most people will only have one dominant wing. (*Dominant* meaning you exhibit more of the behaviors of one wing than the other wing.) It is possible to have equal wings or no wing at all, but this is rare.

+ Your dominant wing number can change from one to the other throughout your life, but it's speculated this might only happen once.

As you read through this book, we will go over what an Enneagram One looks like with both of its wings. If you're struggling to figure out what your core number is, this book series could really help give you some more in-depth options!

HOW DO YOU BECOME YOUR TYPE?

Personality is a kind of shield we pick up and hide behind. It is functional, even protective at times, but altogether unnecessary because God made us in His image from the start. However, we cling to this personality like it's our key to survival, and nothing has proven us wrong so far. It's the only tool we've ever had, and the shield has scratches and dents to prove its worth.

Not all parts of our personality are wrong or bad, but by living in a fallen, sinful world, we all tend to distort even good things in bad ways. Amen?

What personality did you pick up in childhood? If you're reading this devotional, then you may have chosen type One. Your need to be good became the one thing that your life revolved around from early childhood until right now, at this very moment.

The Enneagram talks about childhood wounds and how we pick up a particular shield as a reaction to these wounds. However, not all siblings have the same Enneagram type even though they heard the same wounding message or had the same harmful experiences growing up. This is because we are born with our own unique outlook on the world, and we filter everything through that outlook. You and your siblings may have heard the same things, but while you heard, "You're only loved when you're helping," your sibling heard, "You're only loved when you're successful." Thus, you both would become different Enneagram types.

Trauma and abuse of any kind can definitely impact your choice of shield as well. If you think of all these nine shields as being a different color, perhaps you were born predisposed to be more likely to pick blue than red. However, in a moment of early trauma, you might have heard someone shouting, "Pick black! Black is the only option!" Thus, you chose black instead of blue, which would've been your own unique reaction to your life circumstances. It's hard to say how these things happen exactly, especially when trauma is involved. Are you who you are *despite* trauma…or because of it? Only God knows, but there is healing and growth to be found either way.

We've all heard the phrase, "You can't teach an old dog new tricks." I'd like to propose that when referencing personality, it might be said, "The longer you use your personality, the harder it is to see its ineffectiveness." It's not impossible for an older person to drastically change for the better, but it will be harder for them to put down what has worked for them for so long. That's why, as we age, it can become harder to even see where our personality ends and our true self begins. Even if the unhealthy parts of our personality have been ineffective, they still seem to be the only things that have worked for us.

WHY WOULD WE NEED THE ENNEAGRAM WHEN WE HAVE THE HOLY SPIRIT AND THE BIBLE TO GUIDE US?

The Enneagram is a helpful tool, but only when it is used as such. The Enneagram cannot save you—only Jesus can do that.

However, God made us all unique, and we all reflect Him in individual ways. Learning about these unique reflections can encourage us, as well as point us toward our purposes. The Enneagram also reveals the sin problems and blind spots you may unknowingly struggle with. Revealing these blind spots leads us to repentance and change before God.

HOW DO I CHANGE MY MORE NEGATIVE BEHAVIORS?

Alcoholics Anonymous was really on to something when they called their first step "admitting you have a problem." How do you solve a problem if you don't know you have one or are in denial about it? You can't. If you have a shield you're using to protect yourself from the world, but are blissfully unaware of its existence, you won't understand how its very existence impacts you and your relationships. You definitely won't be putting that battered but battle-tested shield of a personality down anytime soon.

Similar to the wisdom of admitting one has a problem before recovery can begin, the Enneagram proposes self-knowledge as the starting point before there can be change.

Whether you're 100 percent sure you are a One, or just curious about the possibility, this is what it looks like to be a One.

WHAT IT MEANS TO BE A PERFECTIONIST

From the time Peter was a little boy, he was an observer and followed the rules. His bed was made at an age when his siblings wouldn't have even attempted the feat. He colored inside the lines, and he was even correcting his older siblings' behavior. Yes, Peter felt much different than most kids his age.

This was very clear after an incident at his school where Peter, always following rules to the letter, corrected a boy who was blatantly disobeying a clear instruction given by the teacher. In turn, the boy told on Peter—as the correction, I'm sure, made him feel bad. This tattling would cause Peter to get into trouble. Throughout the entire ordeal, Peter's parents could see that their son, and his unique gifts, were not being appreciated or respected in this instance by either the teacher or the school. Peter was right, this boy did disobey a rule, so why was Peter the one getting in trouble? The way this incident was handled was problematic enough that they decided to pull him out of that school.

After learning about the Enneagram, it didn't take Peter long to realize that he was an Enneagram One.

Enneagram Ones are motivated by being good or having integrity. This motivation leads them to follow strict guidelines or rules about how to live life in a good way. If they don't follow these self-imposed rules—or, sometimes, rules imposed by others—then their inner critic fires up a relentless internal punishment.

What's an inner critic? It's an internal voice that sounds like this:

I can't believe you just did that!

Ugh, you're such a screw-up!

You need to try harder. You can't be making mistakes like this.

An inner critic is unique to Ones in the way that this voice is trying to be a helpful reminder to keep them in line with their own motivation to *be good,* but the inner critic is often sorely mistaken on what actions are deserving of internal punishment.

To the inner critic, lying might internally be worthy of the same amount of shame as accidentally breaking a coffee mug, or getting a sunburn might be just as big of a mistake as crashing the car.

The rules that a One feels compelled to hold on to are as different as each individual One. Some Ones might feel like being efficient and quick at getting work done is good, whereas another One holds to a strict cleaning or eating regime in order to feel good.

Despite the inner critic, and a list of rules longer than their arm, Ones are very thoughtful, friendly, considerate, and honest. They want their loved ones to feel safe and cared for in the best way, and they take the utmost responsibility in their work life.

When Ones are unhealthy, their internal criticism can seem to extend outward to be critical of everyone and everything in their path. Their focus will constantly be on what's wrong, and they'll have a boiling frustration that makes them hard to be around.

On the other hand, a healthy One will have a more relaxed approach to life. Using their gifts to be problem-solvers in a world full of problems, they will check their inner critic's voice against what God says about them and be much more self-forgiving, which in turn makes them much more forgiving of others.

ALL ABOUT BEING A ONE

MOTIVATION

*To be good, have integrity,
and achieve this by following the rules*

BIGGEST FEAR

Being evil or corrupt

Ones fear being unable to do good things or make a difference. They fear losing respect from those they love and admire, and overall having nothing bigger than themselves worthy of living for.

GUT TRIAD

Each Enneagram type is dominant in either feeling, thinking, or doing. These *triads* are referred to as heart-centered, head-centered, or gut-centered.

Ones, along with Eights and Nines, are considered to be part of the gut triad. Being part of the gut triad means that Ones, Eights, and Nines receive information through their gut, which in layman's terms means a bodily feeling of something being instinctively right or wrong. A person who has a dominant gut instinct doesn't need to think something over or consult their feelings in order to know what is right. This gut instinct is something unique to these three numbers, and dominance in this instinct is something only they experience.

Each of the three triads has a defining emotion connected to the center they use most.

For the gut triad, this emotion is anger. Anger is like a fire that keeps this triad going, whether they're aware of it or not. Ones, Eights, and Nines struggle with anger, usually over the things that to them are obviously right or wrong. Injustice, marginalization, bullying, and a host of other issues that come from living in a sinful world are more than enough for this triad to struggle with persistent anger, especially as they receive all of this information through their gut. The obvious right and wrong can't be logically (through the head) or emotionally (through the heart) put out of sight.

Ones use their gut to discern what is the good and right way to live. When they see others blatantly disobeying the *rules* that are very obvious to them, it triggers the anger response. It can cause Ones to live their lives burdened by boiling frustration.

CHILDHOOD WOUND

The wounding message Ones heard (or thought they heard) in childhood is, "It is not okay to make mistakes," or "You're only as good as your behavior." This impacts them for the rest of their lives by creating an *inner critic* that chastises them anytime they make a mistake or do something wrong.

A One might've heard this wounding message if a parent or guardian punished them harshly for a mistake, punished them for something they didn't do, <u>had unrealistic expectations for</u> <u>their age or disposition</u>, or otherwise <u>communicated that mis-</u> <u>takes resulted in the One being seen as a *bad* boy or girl.</u>

THE LOST CHILDHOOD MESSAGE ONES LONG TO HEAR

"You Are Good"

These words take the weight of *being good* off of the One's shoulders. As Christians, we believe Christ was the only truly *good* human who ever lived, and through His death, in our place, God now sees us through Christ's clean record.

DEFENSE MECHANISM

Reaction Formation

This <u>defense mechanism looks like feeling one way very</u> <u>strongly, but displaying the opposite emotion outwardly.</u> Usually, this can happen because the One knows <u>their initial feeling is</u> *wrong* or *bad* in some way, so they choose to fake the *right* reaction.

For instance, this can happen if a coworker gets a big promotion that the One knows they do not deserve. Instead of displaying disgust or anger, they will almost overly congratulate their coworker in an effort to have the right response.

WINGS

A wing is one of the numbers on either side of your Enneagram number that adds some *flavor* to your type. You'll still be your core number in essence, but your wing can impact a lot of your behaviors.

One with a Two Wing (1w2)

A One with a Two wing is born to help, and help in the right way. They're friendly, kind, and altogether just a good person, so it might be hard to think that these 1w2s have a bit of a manipulative streak...but it's true. While Ones have *rules* they uphold in general, a 1w2 will also have many social/relationship rules. If you happen to break one of these rules, a 1w2 is very unlikely to give you a second chance. A 1w2 can react almost like an Eight when they see a loved one being treated unjustly. You don't want to be on this anger-triad sweetheart's bad side.

One with a Nine Wing (1w9)

A Nine wing brings some chill to a One's *do everything right now* nature. A 1w9 will be a little more socially aware than your average One, but less eager to please than a Nine. A 1w9 will tell you what they think, coming across very confidently, but may in fact be nervous about the aftermath of their forthrightness. Responsible, loyal, and eager to please, a 1w9 will definitely leave a mark on their circle of influence.

ARROWS

The arrows are the two numbers your number is connected to in the Enneagram diagram. These two arrows represent the number from which you get the best traits as you grow, or the number from which you get the worst traits when you're in seasons of stress.

Stress: Going to Four

In stress, the emotional evenness of a One is flipped upside down when they go to Four. Normally logical, dutiful, and hard to slow down, Ones will become moody, snippy, and almost impossible to cheer up.

Growth: Going to Seven

In growth, put-together Ones can be surprisingly fun as they go to Seven. A normally stoic One will appear to be happy, playful, and spontaneous when that Seven energy starts to take over. As these Ones grow, they will become less critical of themselves and others, and take life a little less seriously.

TYPE ONE SUBTYPES

When we talk about subtypes and the Enneagram, we are referring to three relational instincts we all have. These instincts, like those of *fight or flight*, are reactions over which we have little control. The three relational subtypes are Self-Preservation (Sp), Social (So), and One-to-One (Sx). We all have the capacity to use all three of these instincts, but one of them is usually dominant. That dominant subtype can strongly impact how your distinct Enneagram type looks to the rest of us.

✕ The Perfectionist One (Sp)

Ones who have a dominant self-preservation instinct are true perfectionists. Their inner critic is hard at work on their appearance, finances, eating habits, etc. These Ones are not as critical of others as they are of themselves. The Enneagram worldwide calls this subtype "either highly anxious or highly self-controlled."

The Teacher One (So)

Ones with a dominant social instinct take their perfectionist angst and use it to teach others. By both being an example and physically teaching others how to do something *the right way*, these Ones focus more on their place within social circles and are generally much more friendly and laid back than the other two subtypes.

The Zealot One (Sx)

Ones with a dominant one-to-one instinct are the reason we hear of Ones being *the reformers*. They're also the reason some Ones can look like Eights. Feeling secure in their one or two intimate relationships, this One looks outward at boldly improving the world around them. This One is more likely to express anger outwardly than the other two subtypes.

SO I'M A ONE. WHAT NOW?

Why should I, as a type One, embark on sixty days of devotions?

If you have just realized you are a type One on the Enneagram, or have come to terms with that reality, you've probably thought at one point or another, *Okay, but what now? I get that I'm a perfectionist. I struggle with criticism, I have high standards for myself and others, I value being seen as good, and I have an inner critic whose voice I hear almost non-stop. The question is, how do I take this self-awareness and turn it into practical transformation?*

Some Enneagram teachers will tell you that you need only to focus on self-actualization and pull yourself up by your proverbial bootstraps to grow out of your worst behaviors. They say things like, "Meditate!" or "Focus on yourself!" or "Stop listening to your inner critic!"

However, I'm here to offer a different foundation for growth. As Christians, we know that we are flawed, sinful, and far from God's intended plan for humanity. The hymn "Come Thou Fount of Every Blessing" includes the lyrics, "Prone to wander, Lord, I feel it." This speaks to the reality of our hearts and their rebellious nature toward our Savior.

This wandering is the problem, sin is the problem, and *we* are the problem! So, anyone who tells us that we ought to focus on ourselves to find growth will only lead us to more confusion. We may even find ourselves back where we started, as we go around and around this idea of focusing on self.

But we are not without hope. Philippians 1:6 says, *"I am sure of this, that he who began a good work in you will bring it to completion at the day of Jesus Christ."* On the very day you acknowledged Jesus as your Savior, repented from your sin, and dedicated your life to Him, He began a good work in your life. This work is called sanctification, which is the act of becoming holy. Your sanctification will not be finished here on earth, but you are in the process of *becoming*, day by day, moment by moment, only by the Holy Spirit's work and power within you.

We might not know how to articulate it, but this work of sanctification is the growth and change we long for. All of us know we are not who we want to be. Reflecting on the human condition in Romans 7:15, Paul said, *"For I do not understand my own actions. For I do not do what I want, but I do the very thing I hate."* Isn't that the truth? I don't want to be angry, but in a world full of flaws, my anger has marked more days than I care to share.

We all know we have this haunting *potential* that always seems just a little out of reach. We all have this nagging feeling that we were created for more...but how do we get there? Only by God's grace and power within us can we rest in His sanctifying work and trust Him for the growth and potential of bringing glory to Him day by day. Only God can sanctify us, but it is our responsibility to be *"slaves of righteousness"* (Romans 6:18) and obey Him.

Over the next sixty days, we want to take you day by day through what God says about *your specific problems as a One* and how He wants to lovingly sanctify you into being more like Jesus.

The lens of the Enneagram gives us a great starting point for your specific pain points and strengths. We will use those to encourage you in the areas that God is reflected through you and in the areas that you need to lay down your instincts and let Him change you.

Some of these topics might be hard, but we hope that you'll let the tension you feel in your heart open you up to change. This is where our obedience comes in. We all have blind spots and areas we are more comfortable leaving in the dark, but God desires so much more for us. So ask Him to help you release your grip on those areas, bring them into the light, and experience the freedom of repentance.

I see opportunity.
I see potential growth.
I see right from wrong easily.

I judge quickly and I feel intuitively.
I have gut feelings and I trust them.
I see vision for what things could be.

I like structure.
I like routine.
I like equality and justice.

I see others' needs.
I feel responsible for them.
I feel the need to justify.

In my head, I hear a voice telling me,
You could do better.

That's not good enough.
Try harder next time.

I used to be immune to the voice in my head.
I didn't recognize that it was just a voice, not my identity.
This voice will always be a part of me,
So now I've friended it.
My inner voice is there to help me; it's trying to protect me.
We get along better now because we're friends.

I reflect the Lord's goodness and
I bring Him glory and honor by following His will.
I'm thankful for the characteristics the Lord has gifted me.
I am a One.

—*Lydia Sergio*

YOUR GUIDES FOR THIS JOURNEY

You'll be hearing from another writer and Enneagram coach in the days ahead. The days in which no author is listed are written by me, Elisabeth Bennett. On other days, I have asked an Enneagram expert, who is also a One, to help you on your path.

LYDIA SERGIO

Lydia is an Enneagram coach, essential oils fanatic, and a leader in her local church. Lydia is also an Enneagram 1w2 and has graciously poured out her heart to help her fellow Ones find Jesus and growth in this devotional. She hopes that by clinging to God's goodness, your soul will find peace and joy in Him. Lydia recently married, and she is living her best life with her husband Matt and poodle Stella.

10 DAYS OF GOODNESS

How You Uniquely Reflect Christ

● ● ● ● ● ● ● ● ● ● ● ● **DAY 1**

God's Goodness

And God said, "Behold, I have given you every plant yielding seed
that is on the face of all the earth, and every tree with seed in its
fruit. You shall have them for food. And to every beast of the earth
and to every bird of the heavens and to everything that creeps on the
earth, everything that has the breath of life, I have given every green
plant for food." And it was so. And God saw everything that he had
made, and behold, it was very good.
(Genesis 1:29–31)

Have you ever thought about how God's goodness is reflected in His design for creation? Every beautiful sunset, every waterfall, every majestic animal, and every miraculous human body was created by God…and He called them all good.

God is a God who cares about good things. He didn't slap us together and say, "That'll work." He said, "This is very good." Everything He made, in the beginning, was very good, and very good is still His desire for His creation.

As humans, we instinctively know when we see God's good design. This is why we feel *awe* or *feel very small* when we see a sunset, or why we get that satisfying feeling when we look at something with symmetry or a very organized design. That's how God intended everything to be, and our soul is at rest and at home in His good design.

As an Enneagram One, you probably nod your head as you read of God's good design. The flaws that have come with sin, death, and destruction may pain you more than any other Enneagram type. You see the impact of sin everywhere and have such a keen gauge for what *good* meant to our Creator. Knowing you do not live in a world that is truly *good* like Eden feels like living with a huge rock in your shoe. It's just hard not to focus on what's wrong. But when you see how *"not good"* everything is, that's an opportunity for you to agree with God about His very good design.

God did not intend for us to live in this painful, dying, not good world. His plan was full of beauty, peace, prosperity, and so much goodness. When we notice and focus on those things that still reflect God's perfect design for the world—things like beauty in nature, happy emotions, foods that thrill our taste buds, good health, and wonderful music—we are agreeing with God on His original plan for us, and we have an opportunity to rejoice with hope in what He has prepared for us to come.

SHIFT IN FOCUS

Spend some time in prayer thanking God for His good design. If these words reflect your heart, please borrow them:

Dear heavenly Father, I praise You for Your good design, and how You uniquely wired me to enjoy and seek this goodness. I pray that You will help me to notice more of

<u>what is good</u>, <u>rather than what is wrong today</u>, and that <u>my heart would rejoice</u> as I agree with You about what is good. Amen.

Exercise: Use your five senses to notice what is good around you:

God, thank You for designing ___Fruit___
which is good, and I can enjoy its taste.

God, thank You for designing ___Clean air___
which is good, and I can enjoy its smell.

God, thank You for designing ___Soft cotton___
which is good, and I can enjoy its feel.

God, thank You for designing ___Starry sky___
which is good, and I can enjoy seeing it.

God, thank You for designing ___Bird song___
which is good, and I can enjoy hearing it.

DAY 2 • • • • • • • • • • •

How You Reflect God's Goodness

Then God said, "Let us make man in our image, after our likeness."
(Genesis 1:26)

Dear One, do you know that you uniquely reflect God? In Genesis, God says that He made us in His image. Now, this doesn't mean our bodies look like His, but we reflect His image by reflecting parts of God's character. It's not a perfect reflection; in fact, it's rippled and marred. However, a familiarity, a family resemblance, is still plainly evident between God and His creation.

God is so mighty, majestic, and perfect that none of us can reflect every part of Him, so we see His attributes scattered throughout the entire population. All of us are reflecting Him in unique and very important ways. This is why we hear about each of us being a part of God's "body" in 1 Corinthians 12:27, Romans 12:5, and Ephesians 5:30. Each of us is uniquely made for a divine purpose; each of us would be lost without others.

As a One, you reflect our Father's desire for goodness, His perfection, His integrity, His desire for justice, His desire for truth, and His self-control, just to name a few attributes. These are characteristics of God that your soul recognizes, runs toward, and acts in, especially when you're healthy.

When you act out of your desire for goodness, have self-control, or choose integrity over your own gain, you're often showing the world a part of God that brings glory to

Him. Showing the world the very nature of God is the greatest honor we inherit as part of His creation. As Christians, this is our very purpose.

I find that it's easy to focus on the ways we *don't* reflect God. Our sin is often so loud and shameful, it demands center stage in the thoughts we have about ourselves.

However, have you ever thought about how dwelling on how you reflect God brings glory to Him?

Like a good father who brags about his child's musical talent that mirrors his own, God is proud and delighted in the ways we are similar. Thinking about these things, and thanking Him for them, help us to have the right attitude toward ourselves as humans. We are humble, small, fickle, and sinful. And yet we are also adopted, created, and loved beyond measure.

SHIFT IN FOCUS

Spend a couple of moments reflecting on and thanking God for the ways you reflect Him.

Dear heavenly Father, thank You for making me like You. Help me to notice more and more every day the gifts that You have given me, and how I can glorify You with them. I want others to look at me and see a glimmer of You. Thank You for helping me do that. Amen.

My favorite reflection of God that I can see in myself is

My compassion   .

DAY 3 • • • • • • • • • • • •

Ones' Desire for Goodness

The good person out of his good treasure brings forth good, and the evil person out of his evil treasure brings forth evil.
(Matthew 12:35)

Dear One, what comes to mind when you think of goodness? An innocent newborn baby…a beautiful summer day…a random act of kindness…a room cleaned to perfection? No matter what your perfect vision of goodness is, this desire for goodness is something you share with all your fellow Enneagram Ones.

The motivation of type Ones is goodness, to be good and to have integrity. That is in essence what makes you a One at your core, the motivation for goodness.

How does this play out for you? What does goodness look like for you? Sometimes, I think it's helpful to <u>replace the word good</u> with <u>something else you think *is good*</u> to help get a better understanding of where your motivation is playing out in your everyday life.

This could be:

- Quick
- <u>Reliable</u>
- <u>Efficient</u>
- Healthy
- <u>Clean</u>

- <u>Polite</u>
- <u>Punctual</u>

Just to name a few. You might find that you are motivated more by these good attributes than simply the word *good*.

For instance, "I am motivated by cleanliness because cleanliness is good."

A problem can arise, however, when you assign morality to words like these. All of a sudden, your nephew who hasn't been taught manners is a *bad* kid, or your friends who don't stick to the same diet that you're on are not doing it *right*. These are the judgments others feel from Ones. Although these are the internal thoughts that keep you in line, most of the time, you're fighting for things that are not a close-handed sin issue. Of course, the antonyms of these words could dip into a sin issue. Being lazy, gluttonous, or mean are sins. But as a One, you need to be careful that you're not swinging the pendulum all the way to the other side.

If laziness is a sin, then high efficiency is the only option. All of a sudden, anyone who is not as efficient as you would like them to be is sinning. And that's just not true, nor is it what the Bible teaches.

Your motivation is a gift, both to you and to the world around you, when you make God the Writer of your rules and the Author of goodness. If you follow what He says is good then you have the ability to make a huge impact on the world

---

SHIFT IN FOCUS

How is your desire for goodness impacting your everyday life? *Pressure, High Standards*

What *good* thing are you tempted to assign morality to?

Efficiency, Politeness

DAY 4 • • • • • • • • • • •

Goodness: A Fruit of the Spirit
By Lydia Sergio

But the fruit of the Spirit is love, joy, peace, patience, kindness,
goodness, faithfulness, gentleness, self-control;
against such things there is no law.
(Galatians 5:22–23)

Goodness is a fruit of the Holy Spirit; as an Enneagram One, we reflect the goodness of Christ's character. As the Holy Spirit works inside us, our character is transformed, becoming more like Christ. Without the Holy Spirit, the characteristic of goodness is worldly. Being a *good person* in today's world is a common ideal, which most would tell you they have achieved. But God doesn't just call us to be good; He calls us to reflect *His* goodness and glory.

God's goodness encompasses compassion, generosity, and discernment. God's goodness is seen in His faithfulness.

God's goodness was evident as He led the children of Israel through the wilderness. While Moses went up to Mount Sinai to receive the Ten Commandments, the Israelites created a golden idol. God became angry with them and was ready to throw in the towel, but Moses went before God and interceded on the Israelites' behalf. And the Lord responded with compassion.

And he said, "I will make all my goodness pass before you and will proclaim before you my name 'The LORD.' And I will be gracious to whom I will be gracious, and will show mercy on whom I will show mercy."   (Exodus 33:19)

God repeatedly showed that He was a good God despite Israel's repetitive sin and disobedience. Although we don't deserve God's love, His goodness abounds.

The opposite of God's goodness is worldly goodness driven by human power. This encourages pride and self-sufficiency apart from God. We see in the Scriptures that the Pharisees had self-centered motives of worldly goodness, and Jesus hated it, calling them hypocrites and worse.

Woe to you, scribes and Pharisees, hypocrites! For you are like whitewashed tombs, which outwardly appear beautiful, but within are full of dead people's bones and all unclean- ness. So you also outwardly appear righteous to others, but within you are full of hypocrisy and lawlessness.

(Matthew 23:27–28)

The Pharisees tried to do good under their own human power. This isn't long-lasting or sustainable because it's done by our own strength and not through God's.

Worldly goodness reflects pride and self-focus, but godly goodness reflects the Holy Spirit's work within our hearts.

When we realize that God is a good and faithful Father, we find that we are called to shine His goodness, which shines through us as believers. God equips us with the fruit of the Holy

Spirit and reminds us to use it. We're called to use goodness in our everyday lives. We are called to be the hands and feet of Jesus.

SHIFT IN FOCUS

Think of a time when God's goodness was reflected in your life. Consider these prompts as you reflect:

How do you share goodness with others?

Are you aware that God has gifted you with natural compassion and generosity?

How are you using this fruit of the Spirit in your life daily? Is this natural or challenging for you?

● ● ● ● ● ● ● ● ● ● ● **DAY 5**

The Goodness of Jesus

And Jesus said to him, "Why do you call me good?
No one is good except God alone."
(Luke 18:19)

You might be a little taken aback by that verse. What is Jesus saying here? He couldn't possibly be saying that He isn't good. And you're right, He is not. He is in fact claiming His deity in this passage by essentially saying, "You think I am good, and I am. But only God is truly good, thus I must be God." Jesus, being the linguistic genius He is, the Word made flesh (see John 1:14), was trying to make His audience think...and what He said is still making us think today.

Is Jesus good? Is Jesus sinless? Is Jesus God? These are the biggest questions of our faith and what separates Christianity from most other religions. It's very healthy to wrestle with these questions if you've never done so before. It's healthy to think through how and why you think what you think. I trust the Bible can give you the answers to all three of those questions.

What Jesus is saying in Luke 18:19 is both a relief and a horror to those of us who are motivated by being good. God Himself said, *"No one is good except God alone."* And although we may agree with this statement, do our actions really show that we agree?

When we get frustrated with ourselves for not being able to do something perfectly on the first try, are we expecting deity out of ourselves?

When we hold others up to a standard of unrealistic goodness, or consistency, are we expecting Jesus out of them?

It's important to think over and weigh our expectations, comparing them to what God Himself has said.

There is part of you that believes you don't have to be God to be good, but your desire for that goodness reflects our Creator, who we know in our very soul *is* good.

SHIFT IN FOCUS

Today is not a light day, but an important day for a conversation on goodness and our ability to achieve it. Spend some time wrestling with your questions about goodness, what your soul knows, and what God says about goodness.

Here are some Scriptures to consider:

"I and the Father are one." The Jews picked up stones again to stone him. Jesus answered them, "I have shown you many good works from the Father; for which of them are you going to stone me?" The Jews answered him, "It is not for a good work that we are going to stone you but for blasphemy, because you, being a man, make yourself God."
(John 10:30–33)

And we know that the Son of God has come and has given us understanding, so that we may know him who is true; and we are in him who is true, in his Son Jesus Christ. He is the true God and eternal life. (1 John 5:20)

No one has ever seen God; the only God, who is at the Father's side, he has made him known.   (John 1:18)

And those in the boat worshiped him, saying, "Truly you are the Son of God."   (Matthew 14:33)

DAY 6 • • • • • • • • • • •

Goodness: A World Thirsty for Goodness

Every good gift and every perfect gift is from above,
coming down from the Father of lights, with whom
there is no variation or shadow due to change.
(James 1:17)

Everyone has a story of goodness they have received from a stranger—whether it's a found wallet that was turned in instead of stolen, CPR on a curb after an accident, someone helping you to your car when you had screaming children in tow, or a passing compliment. We all have had interactions when someone was good to us, without the motivation of receiving anything in return. These interactions make our cheeks flush, our minds wonder, and our hearts swell.

In a world that is full of news of hatred, anger, and crime, I think we have all begun to be surprised that there are still good people around us. So often when we encounter kindness, our first reaction is surprise...but there is a deeper reaction, too. A satisfaction, a budding hope, and a dying thirst that just received a drop of water.

Goodness may feel to you like a lesser way to reflect God; we are all capable of goodness and should try to the best of our Spirit-empowered ability to be good. It may feel like being made in the image of God's strength, peace, or creativity might be more useful. Dear One, I'm here to tell you that the goodness you reflect from our God is something for which the world thirsts.

There are so many things that make us doubt God's goodness, and the reminders God sends us from our interactions with others are often just in the nick of time.

Your goodness, and how it brings glory to God, is so needed. Embrace it, encourage it in yourself and others, and let it shine.

SHIFT IN FOCUS

Have you had a *Good Samaritan* encounter that sticks out in your memory?

Have you ever thanked God for that encounter?

What about yourself? When was the last time *you* were the *Good Samaritan*?

Read the story of the Good Samaritan in Luke 10:25–37.

DAY 7 • • • • • • • • • • •

The Pain of Not Being Good Enough

There is therefore now no condemnation for
those who are in Christ Jesus.
(Romans 8:1)

There is a lot going on in your head, dear One. You may not realize that your inner critic is something unique to you, but no doubt you do know that it's exhausting.

One of the worst parts of being a One—living with an internal critic, high expectations, and lists of *good* things to do and *bad* things to avoid—is that you will continually make mistakes and come face to face with the pain of *not being good enough*.

This is the human condition, and it started in the garden of Eden. Adam and Eve had just one very simple rule, but their hearts craved what they could not have.

The apostle Paul did more to advance the gospel than anyone else, and yet he says, *"I do not do the good I want, but the evil I do not want is what I keep on doing"* (Romans 7:19).

Paul goes on to talk about our old sin nature warring with our new nature that we receive when we are saved. This is a tension we all live with. Jesus Christ is the only Man who did not give in to humanity's sinful nature.

This tension is actually something Satan can use to make you feel like a failure. Like you need to punish yourself, try harder, and let shame be in the forefront in your life...because that's what you deserve. Dear One, if you've been saved, then you no longer need to live like your sin nature is predominant. There is no longer condemnation left in God's heart for you. He is not surprised when you sin; He is just waiting for you to come to Him in your failures and trust Him when He says you're forgiven.

<u>Coming to God in repentance is not hiding your sin; it's giving up your right to punish yourself.</u> Jesus has already died for all of our sins and <u>we have been forgiven.</u>

There is pain and disappointment that follows us as we live with this tension between what we want to do and what we actually end up doing. But don't let this disappointment give Satan a foothold into your heart. Instead, let this tension lead you to yearn for your true home and God's presence.

SHIFT IN FOCUS

Spend some time evaluating how your failures, mistakes, and sin impact your heart.

Are you shaming yourself for these things and forgetting to run to God?

Is there a hidden sin in your life, right now, that you need to bring to the light?

How does the truth of Jesus's death comfort you in your failure and sin?

DAY 8 • • • • • • • • • • •

The Grace in Not Being Good Enough

But he said to me, "My grace is sufficient for you,
for my power is made perfect in weakness."
Therefore I will boast all the more gladly of my weaknesses,
so that the power of Christ may rest upon me.
(2 Corinthians 12:9)

One phrase that hangs over the heads of most Ones is, "You'll never be good enough."

Often, this was spoken to you by Satan, or your own inner critic, or maybe it was physically spoken to you by someone you knew. No matter where it came from, this is a paralyzing fear for most Ones. It's a fear that can cause anger, depression, and a deep sense of purposelessness.

We know from the Bible that we are not, in fact, *good enough*. We are born sinful, flawed, and in desperate need of a Savior. The hope in this reality is that when we accept Jesus as our Savior, all of Jesus's *good enough* gets transferred to us. This is not a reason for pride, but for deep gratefulness and peace. When God looks at you, know that He sees Jesus's goodness. He doesn't see *not good enough* anymore; He sees *the goodness of Christ*.

This is the mystery of the gospel, and it's something that we need to remind ourselves of every day. To think of ourselves rightly as humans, we need to hold both our *not good enough* and our peace in Christ's goodness being enough for us at the same time.

Our sin should not surprise us, our sin no longer defines us, and our sin is no longer something that is being counted against us. Our sin should break our hearts and lead us into God's arms, but it no longer gets to be a chain around our necks. We are free in Christ.

SHIFT IN FOCUS

Spend some time thanking God for His grace and the freedom you have in Christ. If it reflects your heart, you can borrow this prayer:

Dear heavenly Father, I thank You that Your grace is enough for me, that I am no longer defined by my sin, but that You see me clothed in the righteousness of Christ. Help me to remember the reality of Your gospel daily, so that I may live in the freedom of Christ. Amen.

DAY 9 • • • • • • • • • • • •

Your Drive to Be Good and How It Helps
By Lydia Sergio

And let us not grow weary of doing good,
for in due season we will reap, if we do not give up.
So then, as we have opportunity, let us do good to everyone,
and especially to those who are of the household of faith.
(Galatians 6:9–10)

Although having the desire to be good can be tiring, I also find it a blessing. Having this desire comes directly from the Lord. As Ones, we have a gut instinct that helps us discern right from wrong naturally. When our gut instinct* is sensitive to the Holy Spirit, it is nurtured into the gift of discernment. The Scriptures tell us that the spirit of discernment comes from the Lord and is to be used for the common good. (See 1 Corinthians 12:7–12.)

With the desire to be good, we have the opportunity to share our perspective, wisdom, and guidance with others. You may find close friends or acquaintances seeking your advice in their personal lives. People see your desire to help and love the world around you. You have a natural gift to come alongside, shepherd, and support these people. You have a natural gift to see right versus wrong and encourage others in what is right. People are attracted to this reflection of God in you.

In biblical times, a man named Barnabas was an encourager and supporter to the apostle Paul's ministry life. In Acts 11:24, Barnabas is described as *"a good man, full of the Holy Spirit and of faith."* He worked as a behind-the-scenes advocate and walked closely with Paul in sharing the gospel. Barnabas is an example of someone with a desire to do good and support all people without becoming weary.

The Lord has given this gift to you. What a blessing it is to have the motivation to be good! Praise Jesus!

> *Our gut instinct should agree with biblical truth, not cultural influence. For example, a One who is living in a highly racist community might have a gut reaction that tells them that being racist is right, but this obviously does not line up with the truth of Scripture. Having a natural gut instinct can turn into the gift of discernment, which is a beautiful thing that can greatly be used to glorify God. However, this only happens when we allow this natural gut instinct to be nurtured and influenced by the Holy Spirit instead of our culture, upbringing, and other influences.

SHIFT IN FOCUS

Do you notice your drive to be good?

Have others affirmed the gift of discernment in your life?

How is this sense of right and wrong affecting your daily life?

Are you able to share that gift with other family members and friends?

DAY 10 • • • • • • • • • • •

Your Drive to Be Good and How It Hinders

Do not speak evil against one another, brothers.
The one who speaks against a brother or judges his brother, speaks
evil against the law and judges the law. But if you judge the law, you
are not a doer of the law but a judge. There is only one lawgiver and
judge, he who is able to save and to destroy.
But who are you to judge your neighbor?
(James 4:11–12)

Your motivation to be good means you want to help those around you. However, this motivation can also hinder you when you dip toward average or unhealthy behaviors.

I want to be clear that a healthy One's desire to be good is rarely, if ever, a hindrance to themselves or others, but many Ones are not healthy. They may experience this motivation in a less than positive way. This is something that you need to be aware of as a One and keep on guard about in your own life.

Your drive to be good can be a hindrance when you put yourself in the seat of a judge. In the book of James, the Scripture is very clear to point out that we are not the lawgivers or the judges of our fellow man. We are all law doers and should be encouraging our fellow man in obeying God's laws, but not criticizing or harshly judging them in an effort to force obedience.

I know that, as a One, it's likely that you have rarely criticized someone harshly out loud, and even if you have, you haven't gone as far as you were feeling was justified. However, Jesus says that even insulting someone is still displeasing to Him.

> *You have heard that it was said to those of old, "You shall not murder; and whoever murders will be liable to judgment." But I say to you that everyone who is angry with his brother will be liable to judgment; whoever insults his brother will be liable to the council; and whoever says, "You fool!" will be liable to the hell of fire.* (Matthew 5:21)

Being a judge is not only a weight of responsibility that you don't need to carry, but the Bible is also clear that it's not your job. Laying down your right to judge others may feel like you're letting chaos reign, but in reality, it's giving yourself and others the chance to live in grace. By living in grace, you're also allowing your desire for goodness to be good and not to hinder your witness, or hurt your relationships in an ungodly way.

SHIFT IN FOCUS

Evaluate your current health using the scale of:

Grace Giving	Often Gracious/ Critical Thoughts	Critical Judge
(Healthy)	(Average)	(Unhealthy)

In what areas of your life does *being a judge* tend to come naturally?

In what areas of your life are your relationships thriving in grace?

10 DAYS OF KILLING ANGER

How the Enemy Wants You to Stop Reflecting God

• • • • • • • • • • • DAY 11

What Is a Deadly Sin?

Brothers, if anyone is caught in any transgression,
you who are spiritual should restore him in a spirit of gentleness.
Keep watch on yourself, lest you too be tempted.
(Galatians 6:1)

Although the Bible does not mention the seven deadly sins, Christians have known about them for ages. The classification of these sins was first penned by Evagrius Ponticus, a monk who lived from 345–399 AD. This list has gone through many changes over the years, but it has remained a helpful way for us to name the vices that keep us in chains.

Each of these seven sins can be paired with an Enneagram number (with two extra sins to total nine) to give us a better idea of the specific vice that may be tripping up each type. This is important information because these vices are often blind spots to us, and their exposure leads to repentance and greater unity with Christ, which is the greatest thing learning about our Enneagram number can do for us.

Here are the deadly sins early Enneagram teachers paired with each type:

1.	Anger	6.	Fear
2.	Pride	7.	Gluttony
3.	Deceit	8.	Lust
4.	Envy	9.	Sloth
5.	Greed		

This idea of struggling with one dominant sin does not mean that you are unaffected by the rest. I think we can all recognize ourselves in each sin on this list. However, the dominant deadly sin paired with your Enneagram type is a specific tool that Satan will use to distract you and the world from seeing how you reflect God.

The deadly sin that Ones struggle with the most is anger. Whether or not you recognize anger in your own life, I encourage you to pray and give this idea great thought as you read the coming chapters.

Exposing blind spots in our life can feel a lot like ripping off a bandage that we might prefer to leave on, but what's underneath is God-honoring and beautiful.

SHIFT IN FOCUS

Spend some time contemplating and praying about what anger looks like in your life.

Does it surprise you to see this sin printed next to your Enneagram number?

• • • • • • • • • • • DAY 12

Boiling Frustration

For in much wisdom is much vexation, and he who increases knowledge increases sorrow.
(Ecclesiastes 1:18)

The Enneagram teaches us that the best things about ourselves are also the things that bring us the most pain. Our strengths are also weaknesses, which I feel is very true of anything that is a human strength. Only God uses talents, glory, and goodness in perfection.

For Ones, this plays out when your fixation on goodness, and doing the right thing, turns into a hyper-awareness of everything that is not *good* or *right*.

+ Being exceptional at grammar turns grammatical mistakes into eyesores that need to be corrected.

+ Being a great driver makes the driving of others seem inconsiderate or stupid.

+ Being a very clean person makes clutter and mess unbearable.

These are just three examples of how your focus on something good can turn into frustration around that same topic—especially because if *you* did something *wrong*, you inner critic often won't let you hear the end of it, and it's unfair that others get to break the rules with little or no consequence. Yes, this is a very frustrating reality.

As a One, you live with anger toward imperfections, injustices, and *wrong* behavior that you experience daily. However, anger as an emotion feels wrong. It's hard to control, it's big and rash, and it can lead to sinning in anger. So, Ones repress their anger, and instead of blatant, hot, volcanic anger, they experience a boiling frustration that never quite goes away.

Satan uses anger to distract others from how Ones reflect God. It's hard to see the goodness when the frustration, criticism, and rules are so loud. This is why Satan uses anger as a temptation to Ones, making it their deadly sin. This constant temptation is why the battle for peace is a hard one to win in the lives of type Ones.

SHIFT IN FOCUS

What is an area of excellence for you that causes frustration?

Can you identify how you repress anger around this topic?

• • • • • • • • • • • • **DAY 13**

What Your Frustration Is Hiding

I was mute and silent; I held my peace to no avail,
and my distress grew worse.
(Psalm 39:2)

As a One, your frustration is probably not hard to spot. You can probably point to a moment of frustration you have experienced in the last twenty-four hours. But anger is a different story.

What do you feel when you read the word *anger*? How do you react if someone tells you that you are acting or speaking in a way that makes you seem angry?

We view anger with such a narrow lens that it's easy to throw it in the *bad* category and call it a day. However, this is not what the Bible teaches. We are told, *"Be angry and do not sin; do not let the sun go down on your anger"* (Ephesians 4:26). We are not told that we cannot be angry; instead, we are warned that anger is a slippery slope that can lead to sin. Anger in and of itself is not sin.

As an Enneagram One, you are so careful about being good that it's very easy to not want to deal with the complexities of how anger can be good, and just avoid it altogether. Isn't that the safest bet?

The problem is that since you were made in the image of God, you get angry like God gets angry. Maybe we don't get angry at the same things or to the same level, but there are times that you anger is in line with God's anger. Injustice, mistreatment, and sin are all things that make God angry and as His image-bearers, these should make us angry as well.

Your frustration is often hiding anger. Some of that anger is justified and good, but some of it is sinful anger that you're still acting on by being frustrated. It can be hard to spot this anger because you hide it well, thinking *anger is bad*. But if you follow the roots of your frustration, you may find that anger is very alive and well inside you.

SHIFT IN FOCUS

How would seeing anger differently help you?

Can you identify both sinful anger and justified anger in yourself?

What are some things you're angry about?

• • • • • • • • • • • **DAY 14**

Identifying Your Anger
By Lydia Sergio

Refrain from anger, and forsake wrath!
Fret not yourself; it tends only to evil.
(Psalm 37:8)

The journey to identify your anger can be a hard one. Anger can cause shame, and everything inside you may be working together to hide the existence of your anger from yourself. However, this hard journey is altogether necessary for growth. If you don't deal with your anger head-on, it doesn't go away; it just starts coming out in other ways. Here are some of the ways anger might be coming out sideways. As you read them over, pray for an open mind and a convicted heart toward your own anger.

ANGER MANIFESTING AS CARE

Ones often see the needs of others daily and try to fill those needs for them. We feel the responsibility for making the world a better place, especially in relationships. We get frustrated and irritated when our expectations are not met, when others are not meeting their own potential, or when our advice for others is not heard. You might get angry when you look at what relationships cause you frustration.

Do you feel responsible for this person? Are you angry with their choices, or your own inability to effectively influence their choices?

ANGER MANIFESTING AS PAIN

Since Ones are in the gut triad, our anger might manifest in our bodies physically. It took me years to realize that my body was holding anger. A tight knot in your stomach or a sharp pain in your back may be a symptom of anger.

For years, my anger manifested in my stomach and back; I became very sick and uncomfortable because I didn't understand what was truly causing my pain. I thought my body wasn't good enough and I needed to fix it with diet and supplements; in reality, I just wasn't in tune with my anger. Repressing anger was hurting me in ways I didn't even understand at the time.

Do you have chronic undiagnosed pain? This *might* be because your anger is manifesting in your body. If you're not aware of this, the next time your stomach is in a tight knot or you feel pain, reflect on what might be making you angry.

ANGER MANIFESTING AS A COMPARISON

What makes you roll your eyes? Who are you most tempted to judge?

Giving a name to these instances of annoyance, judgment, and frustration might uncover areas where you are in fact angry at yourself.

Do the moms who are skinny, wearing perfect makeup and high heels, drive you nuts? You may be angry at yourself for not being able to *stay fit* throughout pregnancies, motherhood, and life.

Does your cousin—who has more degrees than a thermometer, owns a yacht, and buys your grandma the most extravagant gifts—make you want to break something? You may be angry at yourself for not completing your graduate program, getting the right degree, or getting a job that allows you more financial freedom.

SHIFT IN FOCUS

In which category do you think your anger might be manifesting itself?

How does being aware of this tendency help you?

Try praying a prayer similar to this when you notice where anger is manifesting:

Dear Heavenly Father, I notice my natural tendency to feel anger and hold onto it. Help me to realize my natural tendencies and be aware of what I'm feeling. Please help me release these feelings and let them go. I know You bring peace and healing into every situation, so please replace these feelings of frustration and irritation with joy and love from You. Amen.

DAY 15 • • • • • • • • • • • •

Anger: The Sin

For all have sinned and fall short of the glory of God.
(Romans 3:23)

We all sin and fall short of the glory of God—even those of us who try *really* hard to be good, even those of us who are considered saints, and even those of us who are very wise. We all sin. It's in our very nature, and no one is exempt from sin's grasp. So we are not picking on you when we mention this area of sin that might in some ways be a blind spot for you. Blind-spot sins are the most dangerous because we are unaware of how they have impacted our relationship with God and others. Without exposing the blind spot, we won't repent and change.

Anger *can* be a sin. In fact, the Bible talks more about anger being a sin than about it being something of God. Here are some examples of how the Bible talks about anger as a sin:

A fool gives full vent to his spirit, but a wise man quietly holds it back. (Proverbs 29:11)

Anger is a sin when we let it have the reigns, and we lose our self-control.

Beloved, never avenge yourselves, but leave it to the wrath of God, for it is written, "Vengeance is mine, I will repay, says the Lord." (Romans 12:19)

Anger is a sin when it leads us to take vengeance into our own hands.

Let all bitterness and wrath and anger and clamor and slander be put away from you, along with all malice. Be kind to one another, tenderhearted, forgiving one another, as God in Christ forgave you. (Ephesians 4:31–32)

Anger is a sin when we use it as a weapon to hurt people.

Refrain from anger, and forsake wrath! Fret not yourself; it tends only to evil. (Psalm 37:8)

When it's not controlled, anger can lead to other sins.

We have all been a victim of this sin in some way or another. When parents *fly off the handle,* children feel indignation because they are not being treated in the manner they should be. Others' anger can often cause us to be angry, but if we then use that anger in any of the above ways, we sin in response to others' sin. You don't want to get caught up in this vicious cycle. It's hard to even recognize our sinful reactions when others' sin is so loud and hurtful to us. In fact, holding onto anger because we've felt injustice done against us can even *feel* right sometimes. However, as you've just read, the Bible has very stern words toward anger, and God wants us to put it away from us. This is a command that we shouldn't take lightly. It should prompt us to reflect on the anger we might be harboring in our hearts.

SHIFT IN FOCUS

As you reflect on the sin of anger, identify:

How has another's anger impacted me?

+ Have I been sinned against in this way?

+ How did that make me feel?

+ Am I still angry or unforgiving toward this person?

How has my anger impacted others?

+ Have I ever sinned in my anger?

+ Are there people in my life to whom I need to repent of this sin?

+ Who in my life calls me to repentance when I sin?

• • • • • • • • • • • • **DAY 16**

Anger: the Reflection of God

The LORD is slow to anger and abounding in steadfast love,
forgiving iniquity and transgression,
but he will by no means clear the guilty.
(Numbers 14:18)

As we mentioned during the section entitled "10 Days of Goodness," as image-bearers of God, we reflect parts of His character. As humans, we all have emotions, a conscience, a need for community, and the ability to choose right or wrong. These are all things we gained by being made in the image of our heavenly Father; no other living thing has all of these attributes because they are not created in His image as we are.

Anger, as odd as it may seem, is also something we gain from being image-bearers of God. God's anger is righteous anger. He gets angry over injustice, sin, and things that His very creation cries out against.

The biggest difference we can see in Scripture of righteous anger compared to unrighteous anger is that righteous anger is slow, controlled, and not acted on in haste.

Whoever is slow to anger has great understanding, but he
who has a hasty temper exalts folly.   (Proverbs 14:29)

What does it mean to be *slow to anger?* This is not a three-step process or something that can be taught. Rather, it's a symptom, or a mark, of someone who has been saved by God, obeys God, loves God, and is being sanctified by God.

Being slow to anger is a slow, conscious decision to listen to what God says about anger instead of letting your emotions be in control of your reactions.

Being slow to anger is the mark of someone who has grown in *"the fruit of the Spirit"* of self-control. (See Galatians 5:22–23.) It's a mark of someone who has turned the other cheek. (See Matthew 5:39.) And it also the mark of someone who has a right view of God, knowing that we do not have to take justice into our own hands. (See Romans 12:19.)

SHIFT IN FOCUS

As you reflect on righteous anger and how we grow by being slow to anger, spend some time asking God to help you in this area. If this prayer reflects your heart, please borrow its words:

Dear heavenly Father, I thank You that I get the honor of bearing Your image here on earth. I thank You that I am a set-apart creation and that even my anger is a sign of that honor. I pray that You would grow me in self-control and selflessness, and that my view of myself would reflect my view of You and Your kingdom. Help me to be slow to anger, and to honor You in how I respond to such heavy emotion. I want to be angry like You are angry, and not lose control or use it to hurt others. Please grow me in this, Father. Amen.

• • • • • • • • • • • • **DAY 17**

When Expressing Anger Is Okay
By Lydia Sergio

> *Jesus entered the temple and drove out all who sold and bought*
> *in the temple, and he overturned the tables of the money-changers*
> *and the seats of those who sold pigeons. He said to them,*
> *"It is written, 'My house shall be called a house of prayer,'*
> *but you make it a den of robbers."*
> (Matthew 21:12–13)

A lot of energy comes from anger, and this energy is sometimes good. A healthy anger can prompt us toward action. Think of Jesus's righteous anger, a mixture of passion and vigor directed toward a situation, not a person.

In Matthew 21, Jesus cleared the temple courts because merchants were abusing the space and taking advantage of travelers who needed to purchase animal sacrifices for the Passover. The temple was supposed to be used as a place of sacred worship and sacrifice to bring glory to God. Instead, the merchants used this space for their own financial gain. Jesus became angry because honor wasn't brought to God and these merchants had deceitful hearts.

God is a jealous God who deserves all the glory. He doesn't like to see us worshiping another thing and not Him. Although He loves us, He hates the sin in our lives. His anger is righteous and just.

We need to use wisdom in expressing anger, and not give full vent to rage. A practical example might be if your child is bullied at school, you feel anger with a lot of energy behind it, a wave of protective anger. This type of energy could be directed toward a conversation with a teacher, where you fiercely advocate for your child, or a bully awareness group that could benefit the whole school.

Here are a few ideas on how to release your anger appropriately:

+ Go for a thirty-minute walk or bike ride

+ Try two to five minutes of deep breathing while sitting

+ Spend fifteen minutes journaling your thoughts

+ Clean a closet or a messy drawer

SHIFT IN FOCUS

Do you notice yourself being angry toward another person or situation?

When is it appropriate to express your anger and frustration so that it does not become repressed anger?

Pray and ask God to help you shift your anger toward a healthy space.

• • • • • • • • • • • DAY 18

Controlling Your Anger

But I discipline my body and keep it under control, lest after preaching to others I myself should be disqualified.
(1 Corinthians 9:27)

In general, Ones have a very self-controlled personality. You probably have a natural inclination toward discipline and order, and we all know that inner critic is hard at work keeping you in line. This is why self-control is considered to be one of the ways in which Ones reflect God.

However, there is a vulnerability in the armor of self-control for Ones. That vulnerability is anger or frustration.

What makes you frustrated, dear One? Is it a situation? A person? Is it someone or something over which you have no control?

Are there situations or people disrupting your peace? Are they disrespecting you? In order for your inner critic to not jump down your throat about your frustration, which you may notice it rarely does, you have to truly believe in your heart of hearts that you are justified in your frustration.

Frustration may not feel like something *you* need to work on for yourself. You may think that it's the world that has to stop frustrating you.

However, as we've discussed, this frustration can be misplaced anger—an anger that, in many ways, has named you as judge, jury, and executioner. Your inner critic will allow the frustration, but anything further would be wrong, which is why the frustration itself doesn't feel all that wrong. Your inner critic knows that frustration is the dam that is holding back the rushing tides of anger.

But what is that frustration showing about the state of your heart? Your frustration might be betraying your pride, your selfishness, or your anger more than you think it is.

Frustration might feel like a relief, but simmering frustration is not really processing anger the way it should. Your frustration may not be as harmless as you assume.

SHIFT IN FOCUS

What does self-control in your frustration look like for you?

Do you believe God can help you with your simmering frustration?

What are some things that help you when you're feeling frustrated?

• • • • • • • • • • • • **DAY 19**

Hiding Your Anger
By Lydia Sergio

Therefore, having put away falsehood, let each one of you speak the
truth with his neighbor, for we are members one of another.
Be angry and do not sin; do not let the sun go down on your anger,
and give no opportunity to the devil.
(Ephesians 4:25–27)

A One's anger manifests as frustration, resentment, or irritation. As Ones, we have a natural tendency to hide our anger because it's not seen as *good*. This is *repressed anger*. Sometimes, we don't even know that we're trying to stifle our anger! Typically, Ones believe anger is *wrong* and therefore must be kept under control. They may not be fully aware of how their anger comes across, but it is readily apparent to others. Sometimes, Ones can seem to be very uptight and determined, physically clenched, and tight-lipped when we are subconsciously expressing our anger or frustration.

Think of repressed anger like a full kettle of boiling water on a stove: at first, the bubbling is small and unnoticeable. As time goes on, the water inside the kettle cannot be contained anymore because it's boiling so furiously. Eventually, the pressure becomes too great and the lid might fly off, leading to an explosion of hot water everywhere.

My friend had a roommate who took in a stray cat. My friend mentioned she wasn't comfortable with the idea, but the roommate kept the cat anyway. For the next ten months, my friend said nothing, but held in her anger. Then one day, she finally confronted the roommate. That was the end of their friendship. Had she told her roommate she was upset in the beginning, rather than suffering in silence, this confrontation could have been smoother.

If my friend had recognized her anger, instead of repressing it, she would have been able to express it with more self-control. Being honest about how we feel is often a good choice, but we first need to be aware of what we are feeling.

Satan wants you to continue to hide your anger because he knows it can eventually grow so big that you lash out in hatred and sin. But Jesus calls us to abide in peace with Him. The closer we are to Jesus, the more this blind spot in our life will be brought to the light.

SHIFT IN FOCUS

Do you notice a natural tendency to hide your anger?

Do you often sin in your anger?

Does it make you uncomfortable to think of yourself as angry?

• • • • • • • • • • • • DAY 20

Forgiveness for Your Anger

For the wages of sin is death, but the free gift of God
is eternal life in Christ Jesus our Lord.
(Romans 6:23)

Part of this growth in defeating the grip of anger is being able to fully trust and fall back on God's forgiveness. Your anger does not have a hold on you that cannot be broken by Jesus Christ.

Fully revealing your anger might leave you feeling like a bad person, but true repentance and reconciliation looks much more like a reunion than judgment.

God is not surprised by our sin. God isn't waiting behind a corner to punish you for your sin. He is waiting with eager arms for you to come to Him, hands still filthy with sin, and ask Him for help.

I've watched a lot of the reality TV show *Intervention*, and you see this picture so clearly with the parents on that show. They hate drugs, they hate what drugs are doing to their child, and they hate seeing their child in bondage to drugs. But they love their child, and they're prayfully waiting for the day that their child expresses any interest in help. The parents want to help and they would move heaven and earth to get their child the help they need.

This is God's heart toward you and your sin. Yes, it breaks His heart, but He does not see it as a problem that is too big for

His love to cover. He doesn't see you as too broken, too dirty, or too far gone.

> *He has delivered us from the domain of darkness and trans-ferred us to the kingdom of his beloved Son, in whom we have redemption, the forgiveness of sins.*
>
> (Colossians 1:13–14)

SHIFT IN FOCUS

Take a moment to thank God for the forgiveness and peace you have in being able to run to His arms when you sin. If they reflect your heart, please borrow these words:

> Dear heavenly Father, I know "thank You" can never express how grateful I am for Your forgiveness and love for me. I am overwhelmed by my need for You, and I'm ashamed by how I run from You when I'm hiding in my sin. I pray that You would continually convict me of the anger I hide inside my heart and that I would fully trust to run into Your forgiving arms. Thank You for artic-ulating Your great love for us in Your word, and thank You for daily displaying Your love for me in my life. Amen.

10 DAYS OF GRACE
Your Strength and How to Use It

• • • • • • • • • • • **DAY 21**

Grace, Is That You?

> *For by grace you have been saved through faith.*
> *And this is not your own doing; it is the gift of God.*
> (Ephesians 2:8)

Dear One, I want to take you back…maybe to a long time ago, maybe to very recent memory. I want to take you back to the moment you first felt God's overwhelming grace for you.

This was most likely your conversion experience when you first realized your need for a Savior, but maybe it was a recent running back into Christ's arms.

What you felt at that moment was grace. It's an overwhelming feeling that makes you emotional. It makes you feel so very close to God, like the world just got very big and you got very small in the best way.

This is grace: the free and unmerited favor of God, as manifested in the salvation of sinners.

It is *free*, meaning you did not earn it. No amount of good behavior, liabilities, or station earns you grace.

It's unmerited, meaning you're actually undeserving of this grace.

It's from God, meaning that He is the One who gives you grace and saves you.

If you've been saved by God's free, unmerited grace, then you know what grace feels like, even if you don't feel it at this moment. Hold on to that feeling, that déjà vu, as we head into nine days of how God's grace isn't only for the moment of salvation, but it continues and is very practical for you today.

SHIFT IN FOCUS

Spend some time reflecting on the grace you felt during salvation. How would you describe it?

Do you still get glimpses of this grace now? This may occur when listening to a hymn, during prayer, journaling, in church, or having a conversation with a friend.

• • • • • • • • • • • • **DAY 22**

God's Overwhelming Grace

[That you] *may have strength to comprehend with all the saints what is the breadth and length and height and depth, and to know the love of Christ that surpasses knowledge, that you may be filled with all the fullness of God.*
(Ephesians 3:18–19)

Being overwhelmed by God's grace is something I hope you can relate to very strongly. There's a sense of not being able to comprehend the full magnitude or impact of what you're starting to feel. It's a full head, heart, and gut experience.

Most of the overwhelming sensations we feel can be best correlated to drowning or being buried. They're unpleasant to say the least. Being overwhelmed by God's grace is a completely *whole* feeling of understanding your place in the world, a place that is much better than you deserve.

I can't help but think of the book of Job when I think of being fully overwhelmed by God's grace.

At the end of the book of Job, after Job has had his pouting time and is fully wallowing in his depression, God shows up. What God does is obliterate Jobs' poor mood by making him see how very small he is and how very mighty and in control God is.

Feeling small might make you think that Job would've responded by being frightened, but he didn't. He responded with praise, and that is exactly what my heart feels as I read God's words to Job. (See Job: 38–42.)

Dear One, when you feel the overwhelming smallness of being fully known, fully loved, and fully forgiven by God, it humbles your heart to a position where it can't rise to be judge, jury, and executioner. This is the feeling I want you to be able to draw from when the frustration, anger, and injustice feels so *loud*. Breathe in, breathe out, close your eyes, and go back to grace. Let yourself be overwhelmed by it.

SHIFT IN FOCUS

Here we are going to practice drawing upon God's overwhelming grace in order to calm frustration:

Step 1: Recall your strongest memory of overwhelming grace.

Step 2: Recall an incident, reality, or broken rule that frustrates you. Let the frustration start to bubble up in your mind.

Step 3: Now that you're fired up, take three big breaths—in through the nose, out through the mouth.

Step 4: Close your eyes and go back to the memory of step one. Let the grace of that moment overwhelm you, and relax your body, starting with your fingertips and going down to your toes.

Step 5: As your body relaxes, reflect on how the reality of God's grace changes your posture toward the things that frustrate you, and pray that God will help you choose to humble yourself in frustration.

• • • • • • • • • • • DAY 23

God's Unchanging Grace

God is not man, that he should lie, or a son of man,
that he should change his mind. Has he said, and will he not do it?
Or has he spoken, and will he not fulfill it?
(Numbers 23:19)

One of the hardest attributes of God for us to fully grasp is His unchanging nature. Change is something we all deal with every day, both in ourselves and in others, in the world and with everything we touch. Change is the only certainty we know, other than God. But sometimes, our experience can make us doubt the very things that God tells us about Himself. We find ourselves living as if God will change His mind, especially about us.

The Bible tells us, *"Jesus Christ is the same yesterday and today and forever"* (Hebrews 13:8).

We have certainty that if God makes a promise, He will fulfill it, and if He says that by grace we have been saved, we are! There is nothing you can do or will do that will make God change His mind about you. Now as Paul says:

> *What shall we say then? Are we to continue in sin that grace*
> *may abound? By no means! How can we who died to sin still*
> *live in it?* (Romans 6:1–2)

That is to say, those of us who are saved don't live as if we are not saved, just because we can count on the forgiveness of God; it's against the very nature of our salvation.

But if you find yourself being overwhelmed by grace, only to wonder if you may someday mess up so much that grace will no longer be there, you can breathe a sigh of relief. It is clear that nothing can separate you from the love that God has for you.

> *For I am sure that neither death nor life, nor angels nor rulers, nor things present nor things to come, nor powers, nor height nor depth, nor anything else in all creation, will be able to separate us from the love of God in Christ Jesus our Lord.*   (Romans 8:38–39)

SHIFT IN FOCUS

Are you living as if you can lose the grace that God gave to you?

Ask God to help you as you try to live knowing what God says about Himself is true, even when we don't understand it.

• • • • • • • • • • • DAY 24

Grace for Yourself
By Lydia Sergio

Three times I pleaded with the Lord about this [thorn], that it should leave me. But he said to me, "My grace is sufficient for you, for my power is made perfect in weakness." Therefore I will boast all the more gladly of my weaknesses, s o that the power of Christ may rest upon me.
(2 Corinthians 12:8–9)

As Ones, we often set high, unrealistic expectations on ourselves, and are frustrated when those ideals aren't met. I'm constantly striving to live up to my own expectations; sometimes, I feel it's all my responsibility. Whether at home, at work, or in relationships, a common thought for Ones is, *Yes, I have expectations. Others may see them as high, but I see them as appropriate for me.*

I often struggle to adjust when reality doesn't meet what I picture in my head. This may lead to blaming myself or others when I'm disappointed or let down. Since we carry high exceptions for ourselves, we often put those expectations on others without even realizing it! Usually our family members and close loved ones feel the immense pressure we put on them.

Read the passage from Paul's second letter to the Corinthians again. As I revisit these verses, I'm reminded of how I'm not fully responsible or perfect. Christ is my *strength*. When we are weak,

He is strong. Scripture tells us to *celebrate in our weakness!* Jesus is the one we should rely on to carry us through. If I rely on my own strength, I'll feel overwhelmed and frustrated—and fail.

> God is our refuge and strength, a very present help in trouble. Therefore we will not fear though the earth gives way, though the mountains be moved into the heart of the sea, though its waters roar and foam, though the mountains tremble at its swelling.   (Psalm 46:1–3)

There is so much peace in knowing that God is taking care of us. There is no need to fear. We will find grace for ourselves through Him...and that's all we need.

SHIFT IN FOCUS

What are some high standards you keep that others might—or often do—find excessive?

What does God's power being made perfect in weakness mean to you?

Are you quick to admit your faults and give glory to God for your achievements?

• • • • • • • • • • • • **DAY 25**

God Is Not an Angry Father

*For the Father himself loves you, because you have loved me
and have believed that I came from God. I came from the Father
and have come into the world, and now I am leaving
the world and going to the Father.*
(John 16:27–28)

There is a theory that if you are an Enneagram One, you might struggle with your relationship with your father. Either he was too harsh or too withholding, had too many expectations, or was not fully there for you when you needed him. Does any of this sound like your story?

(The theory of parental orientations is not one that everyone can relate to, so if this is not your experience, don't let it make you question your Enneagram typing. However, do let it make you evaluate how this might be true of your relationship with your father, even in small ways. In what ways did you not feel like you could go to him with a problem or concern?)

To a young One, this feeling makes your father seem like someone you don't quite trust to protect you, and you definitely can't go to him with your vulnerable emotions. Your father represents rules, punishment, maybe anger, and the feelings of being *not quite good enough.*

Even with that being the case, you idealize how you want the relationship with your father to be, and you keep trying to have that relationship, even if you have to replicate this with a different father figure.

This relationship can impact your relationship with God in two very important ways:

+ You think, *God is an angry Father, like mine was.*

This assumption keeps you in line; it keeps your fear of God very real, and you respect Him. But if this is your thought process, you will never fully trust God with the most vulnerable parts of yourself—most importantly, your sin—for fear of stern punishment. You may even compartmentalize parts of your life so that you can face God on Sunday. This belief holds the holiness and justice of God in both hands, but forgets about the love of God and His yearning for a relationship with you.

God is a righteous, holy God. Does He get angry? Yes, but unlike your earthly father, God's anger is slow, it's perfect, and *it is not aimed toward you.* That's right; Romans 1:18 tells us that God's anger is toward sin and sin alone. When God is angry at your sin, He is able to still love you fully and perfectly; He can still see you with the perfection of Jesus. This is one of the mysteries of the gospel. As humans, we cannot fully *know* how God does this, but we know from His Scriptures that He is fully able to hate your sin, while perfectly and fully loving you.

+ You think, *God is the Father I've always been looking for.*

The flip side of the father relationship for Ones is that the imperfection of your earthly father can make the perfection of your heavenly Father all the sweeter. This longing in your heart can be filled, and your father-child experience redeemed.

I think we see this perfect father-child relationship so clearly with Jesus. Jesus loved His Father, and His Father loved Jesus. Jesus trusted the Father fully, even to the point of openly trusting God's will through His crucifixion. He loved the Father enough to make His whole life about telling others about Him, and was so excited to return to being in His presence. This is the child-father relationship God wants with you! Fully trusting, fully open, fully together, every day. Isn't this beautiful?

SHIFT IN FOCUS

Relationships with parents can be difficult, so thinking about them can prompt a lot of emotion. Give yourself some time to process today's devotional.

Are you closer to seeing God as an angry father, or your long-awaited perfect father?

How has your relationship with your own father impacted this view?

Have you ever processed the ways in which your father wasn't hard or not good enough?

DAY 26 • • • • • • • • • • •

Grace for Others
By Lydia Sergio

When he [Jesus] went ashore he saw a great crowd, and he had compassion on them, because they were like sheep without a shepherd. And he began to teach them many things.
(Mark 6:34)

I'm sure you've realized by now that everyone is not like you. We all view the world around us a little differently. Sometimes that can be frustrating if your spouse is never on time, or if a coworker doesn't have the same expectations that you do.

This is where our call to compassion and understanding comes into play.

Jesus is the ultimate example of sharing grace for others. We see an example in today's verse from the Gospel of Mark. God calls us to clothe ourselves in compassion, kindness, humility, gentleness, and patience because this is what being obedient to Christ looks like.

> *Put on then, as God's chosen ones, holy and beloved, compassionate hearts, kindness, humility, meekness, and patience, bearing with one another and, if one has a complaint against another, forgiving each other; as the Lord has forgiven you, so you also must forgive. And above all these put on love, which binds everything together in perfect harmony.*
> (Colossians 3:12–14)

Jesus clearly tells us that love should be our posture toward our brothers and sisters. No judgment, or fact checking, or standard keeping, or correction, and if they sin, we are to forgive them. Hear me on this: it's hard to do this, but with Christ, it's not impossible; God is known to work miracles amid the failures and weaknesses of His people.

Although we as Ones value high expectations, I'm thankful that others see differently and bring great value to the table. Our friends and family around us have beautiful gifts that may never come as naturally to us. For example, they may see the emotions and needs of others better than we do. Through this, I must remember to stay humble and accept that *my way* is not always the *right way*. (Yes, I just said that. Yes, it stung. Yes, we're growing.)

This is where understanding other Enneagram types can be helpful. You don't naturally see things from their point of view—and guess what? They don't see from ours either. Learning more about your family and friends can be one of the most compassionate gifts you can give them...and yourself.

As Christians, we're called to be the hands and feet of Jesus, working together for the good of His glory. (See Romans 8:28.) Because of this, we must have grace for one another in the midst of learning and growing. Scripture tell us that we're all made beautifully in the uniqueness of God:

> *For you formed my inward parts; you knitted me together in my mother's womb. I praise you, for I am fearfully and*

wonderfully made. Wonderful are your works; my soul knows it very well.   (Psalm 139:13–14)

SHIFT IN FOCUS

Before I jump into something, I'll often tell myself, *This may not go exactly how you've envisioned it. It may go differently than you planned—and that's okay. It can be different from your ideal and still be good.*

What beautiful gifts do you see in others?

How will you practice compassion and understanding toward others today?

• • • • • • • • • • • • **DAY 27**

You Are Not Responsible for Others
By Lydia Sergio

> *By this we know that we abide in him and he in us,*
> *because he has given us of his Spirit.*
> *And we have seen and testify that the Father has sent*
> *his Son to be the Savior of the world. Whoever confesses*
> *that Jesus is the Son of God, God abides in him,*
> *and he in God. So we have come to know and to believe*
> *the love that God has for us. God is love, and whoever*
> *abides in love abides in God, and God abides in him.*
> (1 John 4:13–16)

It's easy to get wrapped up in feeling pressure and accountability for others. Although we might feel like it, we are not responsible for them. We may often feel frustrated when people don't take our advice after asking for it. We may feel discouraged when we're unheard. We may even take the lifestyles of those closest to us as a personal offense.

However, Scripture tells us that we are free in Christ! The kind of freedom that Paul is speaking of here is true freedom:

> *You, my brothers and sisters, were called to be free. But do*
> *not use your freedom to indulge the flesh; rather, serve one*
> *another humbly in love.* (Galatians 5:13 NIV)

Yes, Jesus called us to share the good news with others, but we cannot take responsibility for someone else's heart motivation or actions. Our responsibility is solely for our own thoughts and actions, not those of others. Each must proclaim Jesus is the Savior for them to be saved. In this same way, everyone is traveling at a different pace in this journey we call life. We may not always see it, but God has a plan working for His glory; we are called to be the hands and feet of Jesus, but we're not called to tell everyone the right way to live life.

This can be a hard balance when we love people so much that it feels almost impossible to let them have their own journey to the cross. We see the pain, we see the mistakes, and we see the potential, but none of those things are our responsibility. We have to lay down our own love for these people. As great as our love for them may be, it is less than the love God has for them. Trust God to be guiding and taking care of them in ways we might not be able to see.

SHIFT IN FOCUS

Where are you tempted to take responsibility for others?

Do you pray for the people in your life who disappoint you? Do you pray about your heart toward them?

● ● ● ● ● ● ● ● ● ● ● ● **DAY 28**

God Will Change You

> *Therefore, if anyone is in Christ, he is a new creation.*
> *The old has passed away; behold, the new has come.*
> (2 Corinthians 5:17)

When you're saved, something supernatural happens inside you. Your *old self* dies with Christ on the cross, and your *new self* rises with Him. (See Romans 6:1–11.)

We are no longer our old selves, but are made a new creation through Christ. I know this can be hard to wrap your head around, especially when we continue to act out of the old flesh by sinning. But we do know that what was created new by Christ can't be taken away. You were transformed, you are new, and since you are no longer enslaved to sin, you have the power to resist the devil.

Here are a few things we know about the old self and the new self from Scripture. While reading these verses, reflect on how you were before Christ became your Savior and how you are now that you're saved by Christ.

THE BIBLE SAYS OUR OLD SELF WAS:

Enslaved to Sin

> *We know that our old self was crucified with him in order*
> *that the body of sin might be brought to nothing, so that we*
> *would no longer be enslaved to sin.* (Romans 6:6)

Corrupt Through Evil Desires

Put off your old self, which belongs to your former manner of life and is corrupt through deceitful desires.

(Ephesians 4:22)

A Liar

Do not lie to one another, seeing that you have put off the old self with its practices. (Colossians 3:9)

THE BIBLE SAYS OUR NEW SELF IS:

Seeking the Things of God

If then you have been raised with Christ, seek the things that are above, where Christ is, seated at the right hand of God.

(Colossians 3:1)

Righteous and Holy

Put on the new self, created after the likeness of God in true righteousness and holiness. (Ephesians 4:24)

No Longer Enslaved to Sin

We know that our old self was crucified with him in order that the body of sin might be brought to nothing, so that we would no longer be enslaved to sin. (Romans 6:6)

We see in the verses above that the new flesh is something that both *is* and needs to be continually chosen. We are both new and need to choose to *walk* in this newness. Likewise, we are no longer living in our old flesh, but we have to continually choose to not go back to our old flesh ways.

SHIFT IN FOCUS

Have you ever heard of the transformation from old self to new self before?

Can you clearly see this change in your own life or was it more subtle? (For instance, if you were still a child when you were saved, your old self may have been reined in by your parents.)

If you are not yet saved, I would like to encourage you to read Romans 6 and discover the transformation that Christ desires for you.

DAY 29 • • • • • • • • • • • •

God Will Comfort You

*Even though I walk through the valley of the shadow of death,
I will fear no evil, for you are with me; your rod and your staff,
they comfort me.*
(Psalm 23:4)

Psalm 23 is arguably one of the most popular chapters in all of Scripture. Even nonbelievers are familiar with some of these iconic verses. But as familiar as you may be with this psalm, have you ever really thought about that last line in verse 4?

"Your rod and your staff, they comfort me."

If you've ever seen a picture of a shepherd, or you're familiar with farm life, you may have wondered why a shepherd has a rod and a staff.

The shepherd uses the short, club-like rod to protect the sheep against predators and also to direct the sheep. Sometimes, he may even use it as a disciplinary device against the more ornery sheep.

The staff, on the other hand, is a long stick with a crook at the end that the shepherd can use to hook around a sheep's neck and pull it away from danger, such as an area with poisonous plants or a cliff. The shepherd can also use his staff as a walking stick.

These tools of a shepherd were essential to protect the flock and keep the sheep in line. So why does King David, who wrote this psalm, correlate these items to comfort?

Protection, discipline, and rules are all things that we crave as humans, even when we run from them. As an Enneagram One, you can especially relate to the thought of rules feeling safe. If there are no rules, then how do you know what's the right thing to do? Without rules, we would have chaos. This is the spirit of what the psalmist was talking about here.

God's rules are for our protection. Like parents who don't let their children play in the street, God has rules for our safety because He doesn't want us to get hurt. (See the Ten Commandments, Exodus 20:1–17.)

God protects us from our *"adversary the devil [who] prowls around like a roaring lion, seeking someone to devour"* (1 Peter 5:8).

> *But the Lord is faithful. He will establish you and guard you against the evil one.* (2 Thessalonians 3:3)

God's discipline is for our protection, but is also comforting because we know that if we start wandering out of line or get lost from the flock, God's staff is right there ready to lead us back. He may have to pull us out a thicket by the neck, but He *will* go after us.

> *What do you think? If a man has a hundred sheep, and one of them has gone astray, does he not leave the ninety-nine on the mountains and go in search of the one that went astray?* (Matthew 18:12)

> *My son, do not despise the Lord's discipline or be weary of His reproof, for the Lord reproves him whom he loves, as a father the son in whom he delights.* (Proverbs 3:11–12)

SHIFT IN FOCUS

Reflect on the comfort of God's rules, protection, and discipline. How have these things been a comfort to you recently?

Do you thank God for His rules, protection, and discipline in your prayers? Spend some time thanking Him for these comforting gifts of love.

• • • • • • • • • • • **DAY 30**

God Has Freed You

So if the Son sets you free, you will be free indeed.
(John 8:36)

We have talked a lot about salvation and grace over the last nine days because understanding the grace and salvation of Jesus Christ is vital to your growth as a One. Grace is not going to be a natural mindset for you, both for yourself and others, and the theme of grace needs to be a well-worn path in your heart. We've given you some tools in order to help you pave this path, but I want to encourage your heart in the freedom that grace gives you.

If you were sitting across from me right now, this is what I'd say to you:

Grace is freedom—freedom to follow Christ's commands, but also the freedom not to add to them. You do *not* need more rules than what God gave you in order to make yourself good and right before Him; Jesus has already done that work. Where you park your car, what's on your plate, whether or not your socks match—these are not matters of morality. Being a couple of minutes late doesn't make you a bad person, and neither does that *big mistake* that still brings you shame.

This is the freedom Christ has for you, freedom from the chains of rules and guidelines that you yourself made. If these *good rules* are causing you shame, frustration with others, and stress, then they are no longer good.

Read that again: *if these good rules are causing shame, frustration, and stress, then they are no longer good.*

If your self-imposed rules are not an issue of morality or obeying God, then you are free to let them go, knowing that if you do so, your standing before God does not change. You're still fully loved, fully forgiven, and fully righteous in Christ.

Dear One, this is the good news of the gospel. You are saved, made new, completely loved, and completely justified in Christ. Trying hard might make you feel more in control, but that control is a false sliver of hope compared to the glory and true freedom that Christ has for you.

Grace is your strength because you have to work on it more than any other Enneagram number, both toward yourself and others. This well-worn path in your heart becomes one of your greatest strengths as you mature and are helped by the Holy Spirit.

SHIFT IN FOCUS

Spend the rest of today or this week identifying three rules that God may be asking you to unchain yourself from.

Remember the criteria of a rule that's *no longer good* is:

+ This rule is not an issue of morality.
+ This rule causes me stress.
+ This rule causes me to be frustrated with others.
+ This rule causes me shame when I don't obey it.

10 DAYS OF SAYING NO TO CRITICISM

Help with a Common Pain Point

● ● ● ● ● ● ● ● ● ● ● ● **DAY 31**

What Is an Inner Critic?

And after the earthquake a fire, but the LORD was not in the fire.
And after the fire the sound of a low whisper.
(1 Kings 19:12)

An inner critic is something that is unique to Enneagram Ones, although most Ones do not know this until they have learned about the Enneagram. They assume everyone has an inner critic.

You may have been told that you're "too hard on yourself," "too rigid," or "need to let things go." In every instance in which other people are expressing sentiments like these, they are recognizing your inner critic and calling out its abnormality. But none of those comments actually tell you what your inner critic *is* and what it's doing to you.

The kicker is this: your inner critic isn't another entity; your inner critic is *you*. We refer to it as its own *self*, but in reality, your inner critic is only as healthy (calm, kind) or unhealthy (mean, self-deprecating) as you yourself are. These are your own deep thoughts lashing out against your humanity and how others impact your ability to be *good*.

The voice of your inner critic will sound as unique as you yourself are. No two Ones will hear exactly the same things from their inner critic, but here are some things Ones have told us it says to them:

+ "I can't believe you ate two cookies! You deserve to feel gross."

+ "You're so stupid! No wonder your boss doesn't trust you!"

+ "You should just stop trying until you learn to do things right!"

+ "That was so dumb! Why did you say that?"

+ "Why did you trust him? You know better! This is on you."

+ "Chicken nuggets again! Your kids are going to grow up fat and blame you."

Maybe your inner critic sounds like your dad when he was harsh and angry with you. Maybe it sounds like the voice of your first grade teacher who corrected you in front of everyone. Maybe it sounds like someone you know, or used to know, who has said unkind things to you.

No matter whose voice you have taken on to carry out critiques in your head, being aware of what you're hearing and how it impacts you is the first step to making sure it doesn't drown out what God might be trying to whisper to you. Your inner critic might be loud, but it certainly doesn't get the final say on who you are.

SHIFT IN FOCUS

A practice that can be helpful in identifying what your inner critic is saying to you and how often you hear it is to write it down. For a full day, keep a notepad nearby and whenever you have a critical self thought, jot it down. This practice often feels heavy, and it can be hard to stick to it, but it can definitely help you identify that voice.

If you live with anyone, you can also let them read some of the things your inner critic says to you. This can help them have more compassion for the criticism that is going on in your head, and help them not add to it.

Whatever your inner critic is saying to you, you can rest assured that God's voice is always kinder, gentler, and more compassionate than you'd expect. I love the verse from the first book of Kings, wherein we discover that God's voice is not found in an earthquake or a fire, but in a low whisper. Your inner critic is not your conscience and is not from God...but we'll get to that tomorrow.

DAY 32 • • • • • • • • • • •

Your Inner Critic vs. the Holy Spirit

My conscience is clear, but that does not make me innocent.
It is the Lord who judges me.
(1 Corinthians 4:4 NIV)

Here's a question about the inner critic that I've heard a lot: "Isn't my inner critic just my conscience?" The answer is no, your inner critic and your conscience are very different things.

An inner critic is your own voice in your own head that is corrective, points out mistakes, and almost berates you in order to keep you in check. As an Enneagram One, you may not realize having an inner critic is a unique experience to you and other Ones, or that your inner critic is *not* your conscience.

The Holy Spirit, who *is* our conscience, is called our Helper, Teacher, Interceder, and a reminder of God's Word.

> *But the Helper, the Holy Spirit, whom the Father will send*
> *in my name, he will teach you all things and bring to your*
> *remembrance all that I have said to you.* (John 14:26)

Sure, the Holy Spirit corrects, but He cares about your sin and repentance, not your flaws and mistakes. His first concern is your soul. The Holy Spirit's voice is also much kinder than the voice we might use toward ourselves.

Here are some examples:

+ *You break your favorite coffee mug.* Your inner critic says, "I can't believe you broke that mug. If you had been watching where you were going, you wouldn't have tripped. Stupid, stupid, stupid! Now you have to buy a new mug, and you probably won't even be able to find the same one." The Holy Spirit says, "Oh, man, it's sad to break something you love. Don't get mad at yourself. These things happen."

+ *You yell at your spouse.* Your inner critic says, "See what you did? I can't believe you weren't able to hold it together and not give in to shouting. Now you've really done it. You have only yourself to blame if you get divorced. You're such a screw-up." The Holy Spirit says, "Not so fast. Don't pretend like that didn't happen. Yelling out of anger is wrong. That was a selfish reaction, but you now have a chance to do what is right: repent and apologize. God's forgiveness is bigger than your sin."

Have you ever experienced those two voices and listened to the first because it was louder?

The verse we used at the beginning of today's devotional is a good reminder of the fact that we are judged by God alone. Whether you think you're doing great or whether you're beating yourself up, you don't get to decide the measure by which you are judged. God is your judge; He makes the rules. The inner critic who's condemning you for *mistakes* doesn't get the last word. If God says you have not sinned, you have no reason for guilt or shame.

SHIFT IN FOCUS

Keep up with the exercise from yesterday's shift in focus. Reflect on the critical thoughts you have, and use this chart to confirm which thoughts are from your inner critic and which aren't.

Inner Critic	Holy Spirit
Brings up mistakes	Brings up sin
Shaming	Kind
You need to try harder!	You need to let Me help you!
Brings up the past	Forgives the past
Condemning	Eager to forgive

• • • • • • • • • • • DAY 33

Why Are You Here?
By Lydia Sergio

*My son, do not despise the LORD's discipline or be weary of
his reproof, for the LORD reproves him whom he loves,
as a father the son in whom he delights.*
(Proverbs 3:11–12)

Sometimes it feels like our inner critic is being relentless, but with the Holy Spirit inside us, it is clear God has made us Ones for a purpose. Have you ever asked yourself, "Why is my inner critic here?" I find myself asking this question frequently.

Here are a few reasons why our inner critic is present.

As a One, we're motivated to be a good person. The inner critic pushes us to hold our expectations high. Ones have a desire to be objective, reasonable, fair, and moral. As we have high expectations within ourselves, our inner critic will often sound like a parent or mentor figure in our head, trying to improve us and make us better. The inner critic is a way we keep ourselves in line.

A few months ago, I was putting away a cart at the grocery store. The cart's wheel got caught on the cart rack and I repeatedly tried to force the cart in, but after multiple tries, the wheels wouldn't turn properly. As I was struggling, I audibly heard, "Lydia, that's good enough. Just let it go." The voice was so real, I actually thought it was my mom talking to me. I turned around, expecting to see her over my shoulder, but instead, I recognized it as my inner critic speaking.

Deep down, we fear we are not good enough. Our inner critic holds us to a high standard and puts pressure on us. Because we're attracted to rules naturally, our inner critic is trying to keep us in alignment with them. While our inner critic is trying to make us a better person by following all the rules, we sometimes feel shame as a result.

When you and your inner critic are healthy, your inner critic voice helps you to do the right things without tearing yourself down. Your inner critic is there to help you. Think of it as your friend. It's trying to guide and protect you. God can often use the voice of our inner critic to help us stay humble. Even when your inner critic is loudly trying to help you, its voice does not have the final say about your identity. There is a time to listen to the critical voice in your own head, and there's a time to let it go and listen to the grace of God instead.

SHIFT IN FOCUS

Do you notice your inner critic or are you oblivious to it?

Have you heard your inner critic audibly?

What does your inner critic say about you?

• • • • • • • • • • • **DAY 34**

When Did This Start?

And your ears shall hear a word behind you, saying, "This is the way, walk in it," when you turn to the right or when you turn to the left.
(Isaiah 30:21)

One of the questions you no doubt ask about your inner critic is: why? Why is it picking on me? Why not everyone? What makes Ones so *lucky*?

When asking this question, it makes the most sense to look back to your childhood. It's theorized that, as a child, you formed your inner critic as a necessary tool to keep you from doing bad things. If you, even as a child, were motivated by being good and doing right, then when you learned something was bad, you vowed you'd never do it yourself. The keeper of all these silent vows is your inner critic, and it lashes out with the rage and disappointment of six-year-old you when you don't hold up your end of the bargain.

These vows, often made unconsciously, are as silly and serious as these:

+ "I'll never stain my clothes like my sister does."

+ "I'll always be a careful driver, not like Uncle Bob."

+ "I'll never get a bad grade on a test."

+ "I'll never lose my toys like my cousin does."

- "I'll always speak kindly to my children and never raise my voice."
- "I'll never get divorced like Sally's parents did."
- "I'll never get fired from a job."
- "I'll never leave garbage in my car."
- "I'll always wash my hands so I don't get sick."
- "I'll never become overweight."

You may not be aware that you are still holding on to this slew of never and always statements. However, if you could identify each one of them and pinpoint their origin, it's likely you were very young when you first started making these vows—and you're probably still making them today. There are so many of them at this point that you can't remember them all, so your inner critic is there to help.

You've probably gotten rid of some of these childhood vows by now. The logic of *always* making your bed might be outweighed by the fact that you're no longer the last person out of your bed in the morning, so your inner critic can forgive this lapse in vow keeping. Or even deeper, God might have helped you see something as forgivable that you still fight your inner critic to believe, but you trust what God says.

This all goes back to the basic understanding that your inner critic is there to help, but you don't have to listen to what it says. It can be reasoned with to a degree, it can be re-taught, it can become healthier as you grow, or it can be ignored. You are not chained for life to your childhood understanding of good and bad, mistakes, and malice intent. Going back and seeing many of the rules in your head, in their truest form, as vows you made in childhood can give you a good gauge for when to listen to that critical voice and when you need to ignore it. Your six-year-old self's understanding of a situation doesn't get to shame adult you.

SHIFT IN FOCUS

Take some time to identify a couple of vows *childhood you* made to yourself that you're still living by, or maybe some vows that cause you shame because you've broken them.

What would it look like to trust God to direct you instead of your inner critic? Read Isaiah 30:21 again.

In your youth, you might've needed the help of an inner critic, especially when parental punishment was in the balance, but now that you have the Holy Spirit, your inner critic may sometimes be doing more harm than good.

DAY 35 • • • • • • • • • • •

Will It Ever Go Away?

*So to keep me from becoming conceited because of
the surpassing greatness of the revelations,
a thorn was given me in the flesh, a messenger of Satan
to harass me, to keep me from becoming conceited.*
(2 Corinthians 12:7)

If you did the exercises from days 31 and 32, you may have a list of what your specific inner critic says to you on a daily basis. In some ways, seeing this written down is comforting. These thoughts are not from God, these thoughts are real, and you aren't crazy. But this physical proof of a relentless critic may also be wholly overwhelming and sad, prompting questions like, "Will I ever be free of this?"

This is a question and a heart plea that all of us can understand in one way or another. As a Four, I've asked myself this very question regarding my emotional responses to life. Sixes might ask this about their inner committee of "what ifs," Twos may ask this about their inner shamer, and so on. We all have a thorn in our flesh like the one Paul mentions in 2 Corinthians.

Paul says our thorn serves two different functions:

1. It keeps us humble.

2. It keeps us reliant on God

Paul goes on to say:

But he [God] said to me, "My grace is sufficient for you, for my power is made perfect in weakness." Therefore I will boast all the more gladly of my weaknesses, so that the power of Christ may rest upon me. For the sake of Christ, then, I am content with weaknesses, insults, hardships, persecutions, and calamities. For when I am weak, then I am strong. (2 Corinthians 12:9–10)

No, you may never be rid of your inner critic in this life, but your relationship with it can change for the better. The healthier you become as a One, the more you will be able to filter your inner critic until it starts to become healthy itself. The voice, the pull toward rules, and the self-criticism are still there, but a healthy One gains the maturity and peace enough to say, "Inner critic, I know you're trying to help, but I don't have to listen to you."

Over time, your critic's voice will become background noise, drowned out by the voice of God your Father in your life. Eventually, your inner voice can become a harmonizing echo of what God says about you.

SHIFT IN FOCUS

Spend some time praying about this particular *thorn* in your flesh. If these words echo your heart's cry, please borrow them:

Dear heavenly Father, I thank You that You can use something as hard as an inner critic to draw me closer to You. I know it is Your design that the *uncomfortable* things of this life would keep me humble and reliant on

You, and I pray that You'd keep my heart postured that way. You say Your grace is enough for me, and I rejoice that this is true. Please help me to continually learn and grow to hear Your voice louder than my critic's. Amen.

• • • • • • • • • • • **DAY 36**

How Your Critic Helps

My son, do not despise the LORD's discipline or be weary of his
reproof, for the LORD reproves him whom he loves,
as a father the son in whom he delights.
(Proverbs 3:11–12)

As your inner critic is trying to keep you in line, its voice will not always be wrong or harsh.

In American culture especially, we have a hard time accepting correction. Humility toward our thoughts, actions, or ideas is not the standard, and it's often scoffed at. We are all about pride—pride in the flesh, pride in life, and pride in ourselves. (See 1 John 2:16.) This means that you, as a One, might think your inner critic has no redeeming qualities. But sometimes, we need reproof. Amen? God can use your inner critic to keep you humble and sensitive to His voice.

Self-depreciation, shame, and condemnation are not from Christ, but reproof and discipline are. When you are average or unhealthy, your inner critic will often sound harsh, its voice dripping with shame, condemnation, and criticism. However, when you're healthy, your inner critic is often quiet, or it's agreeing with what God says about your actions.

If you sin, your inner critic is going to pipe up; its goal of keeping you in line is still the same. However, a healthy inner critic will quiet down once the goal of repentance, on your part, has been reached. Once you've repented, any criticism of you for your past sin is just shame, and you know that shame is not from God. (See Romans 8:1.)

A sensitivity to sin, humble repentance, and love of discipline can all be good gifts that your inner critic can promote in you; this is usually how healthy Ones experience the inner critic.

I once had an Enneagram One client who was in her late fifties. She told me she couldn't identify with having an inner critic because if something, even inside herself, was telling her she did something wrong, then she probably had. This woman is a great example of a healthy One, whose inner critic now works in tandem with the Holy Spirit. This woman was humble and gracious; she lived her life pursuing goodness, while fully knowing she herself was not the author of even her own goodness. Her humility was beautiful and spoke deeply of her relationship with Christ.

God can use your inner critic to call you to repentance, to cause you to feel the weight of your sin and lead you back to Him, instilling beautiful humility and growth.

Satan is definitely trying to use your inner critic to shame you, condemn you, and keep you both critical and discouraged. How good God is that He can redeem even your own critical thoughts!

SHIFT IN FOCUS

The Bible has a lot to say about the reproof and discipline of the Lord, as well as the posture of humility with which we are to receive this reproof.

Whoever heeds instruction is on the path to life, but he who rejects reproof leads others astray.   (Proverbs 10:17)

Whoever loves discipline loves knowledge, but he who hates reproof is stupid.   (Proverbs 12:1)

Put on then, as God's chosen ones, holy and beloved, compassionate hearts, kindness, humility, meekness, and patience.
          (Colossians 3:12)

What does loving discipline mean to you?

Would loving God's discipline make you grateful for your inner critic?

How can this make you more sensitive to God's reproof?

DAY 37 • • • • • • • • • • • •

How Your Critic Hinders

Let no corrupting talk come out of your mouths,
but only such as is good for building up, as fits the occasion,
that it may give grace to those who hear.
(Ephesians 4:29)

Now that we've talked about the ways that your inner critic helps you, we have to talk about how it hinders, especially average or unhealthy Ones. Your inner critic is not inherently bad or good, so the view we have of it needs to reflect balance. You need to be able to identify when it's hindering you, and let it help when it's actually being helpful.

Today we are going to look into specific ways your inner critic may be hindering your everyday life and relationships. As you read, try to be open-minded, and reflect on what might be true of your life.

Listening to your critic can hinder your everyday life because:

+ Making mistakes can ruin your day.

+ What it's telling you can lead to self-condemnation or depression.

+ It can make you anxious about trying new things.

+ You waste time trying to make things perfect when they don't matter.

+ It can be almost impossible to make decisions for the future.

+ You will fixate on what's wrong and miss out on joy.

Listening to your critic can hinder you relationships because:

+ Nobody can meet your critic's standards.

+ You will start enforcing your critic's rules on others.

+ It will make it hard to forgive others.

+ It can be almost impossible to get over rejection.

+ You will argue about many things that don't really matter.

+ It will be hard to listen empathetically.

+ You will be very defensive when your rules are questioned.

You may not have thought that many of the statements listed here could be attributed to your inner critic's voice. You're so familiar with it that it's sometimes hard to even recognize when you're listening to your inner critic. Read these lists again and circle the things you struggle with the most. When you notice them in your life, pause and try to identify what your inner critic is saying. Is it helpful? Is it what God would say to you?

SHIFT IN FOCUS

Can you see where your inner critic is hindering your everyday life and relationships?

Is there anything you'd add to these two lists?

If your heart needs some encouragement today, re-reading day 35 might be helpful.

• • • • • • • • • • • • DAY 38

Criticism That Brings Shame
By Lydia Sergio

> *I sought the LORD, and he answered me; he delivered me*
> *from all my fears. Those who look to him are radiant;*
> *their faces are never covered with shame.*
> (Psalm 34:4–5 NIV)

Living with an inner critic in your head can often bring the paralyzing weight of shame. Scripture tells us that when we look to God and ask Him for guidance, He will be our source of comfort and we will not live in shame. Instead, we will find freedom! Shame is a painful feeling that the enemy uses to separate us from God's love. God's kindness delivers us from shame. As believers of Christ, we have access to this kindness, also known as grace. (See Hebrews 12:2.)

Have you ever held your emotions inside because of shame? Just the other day, I dropped a glass jar at the grocery store, and it broke in the aisle. Immediately after it crashed, I felt a wave of embarrassment. I was unsure how to react with the other customers around me, and I wanted to hide. I didn't want to tell an employee about my mishap, but when I did, the shame softened; when I apologized, the shame disappeared.

The love that God pours out on us does not involve shame. God's love is pure, kind, and "*sweeter than honey*" (Psalm 119:103). God does not repeatedly bring up past sin, and He knows what is best for us. Scripture tells us that God forgives us and no longer sees us through the lens of our past sins.

> For I will be merciful toward their iniquities, and I will remember their sins no more. (Hebrews 8:12)

It's an easy habit to remind myself of the mistakes I've made throughout the day. ("I should've been more careful with the glass jar at the grocery store," "I shouldn't have said that to Amy....") But the truth is, that is the voice of shame, not the kindness of God.

In John 4, Jesus approached a Samaritan woman and asked her for a drink of water from the well. Culturally, the Samaritans were despised and considered unequal to the Jewish people. The fact that Jesus even talked to her was countercultural. The Samaritan woman experienced shame every day, but Jesus talked to her with kindness and grace.

Is He trying to speak kindness and grace to the areas of your own shame today?

SHIFT IN FOCUS

What are some mistakes or shortcomings that you're often tempted to shame yourself over?

What does the grace of God sound like to you?

• • • • • • • • • • • DAY 39

It's Okay to Make Mistakes
By Lydia Sergio

Not that I have already obtained this or am already perfect,
but I press on to make it my own,
because Christ Jesus has made me his own.
(Philippians 3:12)

As a One, I'm a perfectionist by nature. Striving for perfection is something I've always pursued, and it's always been my goal. I always want to *be better* and *do better*. I have the inner critic, with thoughts running through my head and telling me things should be better:

+ *"That's not good enough."*

+ *"Why aren't you doing more?"*

+ *"You can do better than that."*

It's easy for me to fall into believing these critical thoughts in my head. More often than not, I don't even notice them, but just accept them. On the one hand, I always want to do better, but better is never good enough. Contrarily, I notice that when I'm healthy and secure, my inner critic is quieter. When I stress, it's louder than usual. Quite honestly, it's exhausting.

The Lord tells us we're not made perfect. We're not going to be perfect in this life—in fact, it's impossible. We're going to fail and make mistakes. That's okay. There's grace enough for your humanity and your weakness.

When we are in Christ, we're made perfect in Him. Philippians 3 is one of my favorite chapters of the Bible, and it's been speaking to me recently. These verses remind me that I am whole and complete in Christ. I'm learning that I don't have to listen to this critical voice in my head. I'm *not* perfect. I wasn't designed for perfection. The Lord made me to be who I am. To be perfect in His image is good enough. There's room for mistakes and grace in that.

> But our citizenship is in heaven, and from it we await a Savior, the Lord Jesus Christ, who will transform our lowly body to be like his glorious body, by the power that enables him even to subject all things to himself.
>
> (Philippians 3:20–21)

God promises to make us whole and complete in Him alone. I get excited thinking about the arrival of Christ! We will be transformed and made whole, perfect and blameless. Can you picture how amazing that will be?

SHIFT IN FOCUS

How do you feel when you make a mistake?

What other Scriptures are comforting to you, and help you understand God's grace?

• • • • • • • • • • • • **DAY 40**

Mistakes Are Not Your Identity

I am the vine; you are the branches.
Whoever abides in me and I in him, he it is that bears much fruit,
for apart from me you can do nothing.
(John 15:5)

One of the biggest lies Satan may use your inner critic to tell you is that your mistakes define you. When he does this, you may hear, "It's not okay to make mistakes. You are your mistakes, and you just need to try harder not to make any more mistakes."

Dear One, this is not God's heart toward you. God is serious about sin; Jesus had to die because of sin. But mistakes are a different matter altogether.

You broke a mug; it was an accident, a mistake. Yes, mistakes aren't fun, and sometimes they have consequences—now you have to buy a new mug—but they're not sin.

Your mistakes are a sign of your human state of being. They're humbling, but they do not define you. Your inner critic will try to purge you of mistakes and psychologically beat you into submission, but as we've seen, this does more harm than good.

You will never be mistake-free, and that's okay. It's a hard practice, even a spiritual one, for Ones to begin to let go of mistakes, both their own and others. This will look like a lot of self-talk in the beginning. It involves reasoning with your inner critic about why you're not upset about this, and refusing to listen if it tries to berate you further.

You can tell your inner critic, *I broke this mug, but it was a mistake. I will buy a new one and it's no big deal. I will not listen to your criticism if you're going to make me feel bad about a mistake.*

You may need to say this out loud at first, then say it in your head. Soon it will become a habitual thought. You will be teaching your inner critic what is true. But it takes work to get there, and it won't feel good. In moments when the inner critic's voice feels loud, you feel accused, and you're trying hard to not listen.

Lean on God. Pray, yell out loud, journal, and vent about how hard this is. You can share this struggle with Him, and He will be faithful to comfort you through it. You don't need to fear Him confirming what your critic is saying.

SHIFT IN FOCUS

Is there a mistake in your past that still brings you pain?

Have a firm chat with your critic about:

+ Why this past event is a mistake and not a sin.

+ Why you will no longer tolerate your critic bringing it up.

10 DAYS OF HANDLING DESPAIR
Going to Four in Stress

• • • • • • • • • • • • **DAY 41**

Seasons of Growth

For everything there is a season, and a time for every matter under heaven: a time to be born, and a time to die; a time to plant, and a time to pluck up what is planted; a time to kill, and a time to heal; a time to break down, and a time to build up; a time to weep, and a time to laugh; a time to mourn, and a time to dance; a time to cast away stones, and a time to gather stones together; a time to embrace, and a time to refrain from embracing; a time to seek, and a time to lose; a time to keep, and a time to cast away; a time to tear, and a time to sew; a time to keep silence, and a time to speak; a time to love, and a time to hate; a time for war, and a time for peace.

(Ecclesiastes 3:1–8)

In the whirlwind of life, expectations, and demands, it can be hard to think of ourselves as living seasonally. We live on an earth with winter, spring, summer, and fall, and we observe and celebrate the earth and its seasons, but we rarely give ourselves permission to change and transform. Instead, we expect all or nothing. Either I am…or I am not. There is *right now*, and anything worth doing is worth doing *today*. This is especially true in the hustle of America.

Of course, as we look at our own life, seasons are evident. There was that really hard year of illness, there were years of singleness, there were those amazing three months of falling in love, there were years with little kids, there were years of learning—everything in its own season.

We have a lot to learn from the way God created the earth with its seasons. In these verses from Ecclesiastes, Solomon notes there is a season for everything, and we can see that he's talking about us, not just the earth. The wisest king who ever lived says that for every bad or hard season we experience, there is a season of rest and good to come.

SHIFT IN FOCUS

In the next nine days, we will go into detail about what seasons of stress look like for you as a One.

As you look at your own life today, what season are you in? Read Ecclesiastes 3:1–8 again and pick one or two adjectives that represent the season you're in. Are you mourning or celebrating? Transitioning or resting? Uprooting or planting?

If you're in a more hopeful, joyful, and restful season, it may be time to press into growth and celebrate the growth you can see in yourself. If you're in a season of hard transition and survival, it may be helpful for you to view this time as a passing season and discover hope on the horizon. You may see some ways that you're growing even in stress and adversity. Celebrate those wins!

• • • • • • • • • • • DAY 42

How Do I "Go to Four" in Stress?

How long must I take counsel in my soul and have sorrow in my heart all the day? How long shall my enemy be exalted over me? Consider and answer me, O LORD my God; light up my eyes, lest I sleep the sleep of death, lest my enemy say, "I have prevailed over him," lest my foes rejoice because I am shaken.
(Psalm 13:2–4)

In light of talking about seasons, I think we all know that there are seasons of stress we walk through. Some are lighter than others, but all bring the anxiety and feeling of trying to survive that's familiar to us all.

When we talk about stress using Enneagram verbiage, we aren't talking about being late for work or losing your keys. We all get frustrated and irritable in those circumstances. No, when the Enneagram refers to going to another number in stress, it means seasonal stress—you just lost your job, you're transitioning, your loved one just passed away, and other harsh or trying circumstances. In those times, you're often in survival mode for months or years.

For an Enneagram One, seasons of stress look like coping by picking up the more negative behaviors of a type Four, the Individualist. You will not functionally *become* a type Four, but your normally disciplined, logical, and calm disposition can take quite the shift during these seasons.

If you can look back on seasons of stress in your life—or maybe you're in one now—you'll likely see these behaviors as a pattern that pops up:

+ A hopeless outlook on your problems

+ A despairing mood that feels impossible to shake

+ Anger or defensiveness when others try to cheer you up

+ Your emotional reactions being bigger than what the situation warrants

+ Little or no motivation to do things

+ Struggling to remain objective or logical

+ Speaking in dramatic language, saying things like "I'll always feel this way," "I hate everything," "Life will never get any better," or "Nobody likes me."

These behaviors, dear One, are a huge red flag that you're in a season of stress. The good news is that *what you're experiencing is a season, and it will pass.* This season, like the ones before it, will change and morph into better times. But acknowledging the season at hand and giving yourself grace for survival will serve you greatly during what can be a very frustrating time.

SHIFT IN FOCUS

Do you believe you're currently in a season of stress?

What Four behaviors do you see most often in yourself when you're in seasons of stress?

• • • • • • • • • • • DAY 43

Symptoms of Stress

Rejoice in hope, be patient in tribulation, be constant in prayer.
(Romans 12:12)

Seasons of stress are hard enough without the pressure to perform like we aren't in them. This is why recognizing your stress symptoms and giving yourself the necessary grace for the season you're living in can be so helpful.

So besides a bullet point list of these behaviors, what does this look like for type Ones? I'm glad you asked, for an Enneagram One going into a season of stress looks a lot like depression, but to the One, it feels more like the overwhelming defeat of failure.

Whatever your season of stress entails, your perfectionistic ideal has not been achieved, and in some way, you blame yourself, even if there was nothing you could have done. Even if you tried your hardest to keep the status quo, or make the right decisions, here you are in this so stressful season. You could not prepare enough, do enough, or be good enough for this season not to be overwhelming, hard, and difficult to manage. You may be blaming yourself for your circumstances, or even just blaming yourself for how you're reacting to them.

This sends you into what could be called a *pity party* that feels 100 percent justified to you. You're punishing yourself, you're coping, and you're wearing your disappointment on your sleeve. In your mind, nothing could change what is happening inside you...so you go with it.

This may last for an evening, or you may slip in and out of this state mentally for months. Your stress is manifesting itself—and it's exhausting. You need to emotionally express what is happening, you need to process what you're going through, and you need to grieve. However, hopelessness and despair are not an effective coping strategy.

Here are three thoughts to cling to as you navigate these seasons:

1. **There is always hope.** Even if everything seems dire, and you don't know what the next *right* step is, where there is life and breath, there is hope. If you are still here, then God is not done with you. There is hope in that.

2. **You do not need to be punished for this.** It doesn't matter what your inner critic is saying, or the list of "I should haves" in your head. Seasons of stress are a fact of life and rarely have anything to do with our mistakes.

3. **God is here.** Clinging to hope despite what you feel means fiercely clinging to God, who is our hope. "*God is our refuge and strength, a very present help in trouble*" (Psalm 46:1). Let yourself be alone, feel all the feelings that are causing this dark cloud to descend, and let God into the mess of what you feel. He's here, He's never left, and He's waiting for you to collapse in His arms.

SHIFT IN FOCUS

Do you relate to the negative behaviors of an Enneagram Four being tied to your own feelings of failure?

Which of the three thoughts do you need to cling to the most right now?

Memorize Romans 12:12: *"Rejoice in hope, be patient in tribulation, be constant in prayer."*

DAY 44 • • • • • • • • • • • •

The Worst of Type Four

So I turned about and gave my heart up to despair.
(Ecclesiastes 2:20)

Fours grew up believing something was wrong with them, that something was missing. They thought, *Why is everyone else so likable, and I'm not? Why is everyone so talented, and I'm not? Why is it so easy for everyone else to become themselves? What's wrong with me?*

Fours are highly emotional people; they receive all information first through, "How does this make me feel?" Then they process that information with further feeling before looking at it objectively or taking any action...if they do indeed get to that point. Fours' emotions are very loud to them. Every other Enneagram number has somewhere to put their emotions—like a backseat, a bottle, or a basement—but for Fours, everything hits the windshield. They have to deal with it. And take it from an Enneagram Four, it feels terrible.

To Fours, being trendy or socially normal can feel like being inauthentic. Fours think that if everyone else is doing it, then they are being influenced and it's not their genuine choice. This inner dialogue gives Fours a bit of a thrill whenever they find out something about themselves that's rare or unique, even if it's their eye color, blood type, or birth date.

Fours tend to have a love of beauty that translates into being quite creative. Creative expression will look different for each

Four, but it is fair to assume that there are quite a few Fours among famous musicians, artists, photographers, writers, and creative people of all kinds.

Why are we talking so much about Fours in a devotional for Ones? Well, since you go to Four in stress, learning about this Enneagram type is essentially learning about part of yourself. When you know more about Fours, their tendencies, motivations, and their pain, you'll be able to see more behaviors that come out in stress for you than we could ever list.

Where in times of stress are you seeing authenticity becoming more important? Do you feel more drawn to creative arts? Do you become fearful that something is wrong with you? All of these things can be manifestations of you going to Four in stress.

SHIFT IN FOCUS

Do you have any Fours in your life?

What do you admire about them?

What do you find difficult about them?

DAY 45 • • • • • • • • • • •

The Dark Cloud

Why are you cast down, O my soul, and why are you in turmoil
within me? Hope in God; for I shall again praise him,
my salvation and my God.
(Psalm 43:5)

Maybe even as a One yourself, you have observed another One going into a season of stress. Being a very dutiful number, Ones don't typically stop all movement or ditch responsibility, but they do operate under a dark cloud in seasons of stress. This is a very real reality for type Ones as they go to Four.

This dark cloud could be called a bad mood that you can't shake, or even depression in the most severe cases. Either way, it's a pretty obvious sign of stress that you may think you're hiding better than you are. This being the case, the phrase *dark cloud* might be a helpful one for you to give the people in your life as a check-in for your stress level.

It will let them know that they can tell you, "You look like you're walking around under a dark cloud. Are you okay?"

You will first have to stop yourself from getting defensive. Instead, ask yourself these three questions:

1. Is something stressing me out?
2. If so, is there an action I can take to relieve some stress? (Make that appointment, have a conversation, pay that bill, etc.)

3. If there's no action I can take, how can I hope in God right now? What does praise look like right now?

SHIFT IN FOCUS

In Psalm 43:5, the psalmist notices his own dark cloud and is preaching the remedy to himself. This verse is an amazing tool for Ones to memorize and keep in mind in seasons of stress.

DAY 46 • • • • • • • • • • • •

How It Feels

My days are swifter than a weaver's shuttle and
come to their end without hope.
(Job 7:6)

Every winter, the clouds hang heavily in the skies over Washington State, where I live. You may assume the notorious rain is what bothers most of the residents here and causes seasonal affective disorder (SAD), but I can assure you that what we *actually* miss is the sun. It's not uncommon for us to go more than ninety days without direct sunlight between the months of November and February.

Having lived here all my life, this doesn't bother me much, but that first day when I see the sun again every year, something inside me changes. I didn't know I was longing for sunlight, but all of a sudden, everything feels easier. Even if it still is raining, the rays of sunlight through my window give me energy, joy, and peace that I didn't know I had been missing all winter long.

This, my friends, is what a dark cloud can feel like in your own life. Stress is sneaky like that. You may feel a hopelessness that begs for your attention and makes you forget what hope, joy, or fun even feels like. You may have eased into this season to the point that it doesn't feel weird to be tired, stressed, or hopeless anymore. You're just surviving and focusing on getting through it.

Maybe this is you today, and it's hard for you to remember what the sun feels like. Maybe hope feels so far gone that it's not practical to think about it anymore. Maybe you've all but forgotten that hope, joy, or fun is even an option.

Wherever you are, and however heavy your dark cloud is, can I pray for you?

Dear heavenly Father, I pray for my One friend and how they're struggling under the weight of this season. Lord, please help remind them that hope is an option, and that You are a God of great hope. You know the plans You have for the One holding this devotional, Lord, and I pray that You'd help them to trust You with what those plans are. Even seasons of survival can be used by You, dear God, and I pray that You'd use this One mightily. In Jesus's name, amen.

SHIFT IN FOCUS

Have you forgotten that hope is an option?

Have you forgotten to long for the sun in your own life?

If you're not in a season of stress, do you recognize these words for your past self?

Consider writing a letter to your future self for your next season of stress to give yourself hope during that time.

DAY 47 • • • • • • • • • • • •

How It Appears to Others
By Lydia Sergio

The LORD *makes firm the steps of the one who delights in him;
though he may stumble, he will not fall, for the* LORD
upholds him with his hand.
(Psalm 37:23–24 NIV)

In a season of stress, practical and idealistic Ones may look overly dramatic and attention-seeking to others. This can be confusing both to you and the people around you.

A few years ago, I was very sick. I moved home after college and my body never felt worse. Everything I ate made my stomach burn and I always felt nauseous. I kept thinking I was a healthy person because I ate all the *right* foods, but I never felt comfortable and I was always bloated. At this time of my life, everything hurt, physically and emotionally. I was working full time at my local library and I called in sick multiple times because things hurt too much to even stand.

I came home crying day after day and slept on the couch because my body ached so much. This was a season in my life where I was frustrated and annoyed with my body. It wasn't an overnight process, but month by month, I started to feel better. Slowly and surely, I'm at a healthier point in my life and I became healed.

Now as I look back, this was a season of stress and challenge for me. Usually a routine person, I found myself binge eating and not exercising. Usually an assertive person, I found myself burying feelings of resentment and anger toward others at college. I found myself stressed and overwhelmed because I was striving to please my college professors. I found myself at the extreme end of what I wanted to be. I remember my mom being so surprised at my emotions and tears. It was confusing to my family because this was so unlike my normal, independent self. It was easy to fall into a pity party and it felt completely justifiable because I was hurting.

Through this season, be in the Word and learn to take comfort in God's voice. Scripture tells us that when we remain faithful, the Lord promises to hold our hand and walk with us in these dark times. When you spend time with the Lord, His voice becomes louder than your inner critic and the enemy's voice.

Don't be afraid to tell those around you the depth of your pain. The Bible tells us, *"Bear one another's burdens"* (Galatians 6:2). Even if you are a typically independent person, this burden you're carrying in a season of stress might be too much for you to handle on your own.

Don't be afraid to say, "I'm not doing okay," and let others help you.

SHIFT IN FOCUS

In this season, do you find yourself distancing yourself from God?

Are you spending time in God's Word?

Reflect on Psalm 37 today.

DAY 48 • • • • • • • • • • •

How to Distract

The thief comes only to steal and kill and destroy.
I came that they may have life and have it abundantly.
(John 10:10)

A lot of Enneagram types find it helpful to sit in their pain and process emotion, even when they don't feel like it. However, this is not always the most useful action for Ones. When Ones go to Four in stress, they tend to get caught in emotional spirals, moving mentally closer and closer to the problem and losing all objectivity. You need to get away from the problem, and one of the best ways to do this is with fun distractions.

You probably already have a couple of distractions you use to distance yourself from issues without even knowing this is going on, or that it's the most healthy thing for you! Our souls often just know what things are good for us, and we latch onto them as God in His kindness reveals what we need.

But if you're a little stumped on what healthy distractions can look like, here are some options:

+ Go for a walk or run while listening to music

+ Watch a movie or show that makes you laugh

+ Run an errand

+ Talk to someone who's fun or easy to talk to

+ Take a shower, get a massage, or get your nails done

+ Go to bed!

+ If you can, book a vacation

This is not a conclusive list, but you get the idea. The hard part is choosing a distraction *instead* of a spiral. Especially as problem solvers, it can feel like torture to leave something unfixed and still emotionally raw, but getting distance from the problem is often the most helpful thing. It just doesn't make the choice and action of distraction any easier. Whatever you're stressed about will likely still be there when you come back…but it may look different once you've gained some objective distance.

SHIFT IN FOCUS

Do you already have distractions in place in your life to help you when you're emotionally spiraling?

If not, what are three distracting things or actions that you enjoy that you can keep in mind for the next time you need them?

DAY 49 • • • • • • • • • • •

How to Calm Your Mind
By Lydia Sergio

Draw near to God, and he will draw near to you.
(James 4:8)

When I'm in a season of stress, I often spend a lot of time reflecting. When I'm restless, this tells me I'm not in agreement with the Lord. The Lord brings peace. (See Colossians 3:15.) When I'm not filled with peace, I'm not fully engaged in His presence, which means I need to spend more one-on-one time with Him.

Scripture tells us that the closer we are to Jesus, the closer we will feel Him in return. This is a natural tendency in a relationship. The more time we spend with someone, the closer we become to that person. The more we feel secure, safe, and trusted with that person, the better the relationship. God wants our hearts. (See Matthew 22:37.) He wants to spend time with us and He wants us to draw near to Him.

When I'm in a closer relationship with Jesus, I'm a healthier person; I'm more fun and relaxed. My mind is free, my spirit is filled with peace and joy, and my heart is full of love and grace. It's easier for me to make good decisions and not listen to my inner critic's voice.

To experience the freedom and peace of Jesus, I spend time with Him. I spend time drawing near to Jesus through worship, prayer, and journaling. I read His Word—the book of John is one of my favorite places to start—and meditate on Scripture. I memorize His words and hide them in my heart because what's hidden in our hearts bubbles over naturally. (See Proverbs 4:23.)

> *I have stored up your word in my heart, that I might not sin against you. Blessed are you, O LORD; teach me your statutes! With my lips I declare all the rules of your mouth. In the way of your testimonies I delight as much as in all riches. I will meditate on your precepts and fix my eyes on your ways. I will delight in your statutes; I will not forget your word.*   (Psalm 119:11–16)

SHIFT IN FOCUS

Are you currently in a close relationship with the Lord or a distant one?

How are you going to draw closer to Him?

DAY 50 • • • • • • • • • • •

How to Find Joy
By Lydia Sergio

Consider it pure joy, my brothers and sisters, whenever you face
trials of many kinds, because you know that the testing of your faith
produces perseverance. Let perseverance finish its work so that you
may be mature and complete, not lacking anything.
(James 1:2–4 NIV)

When you're in a season of stress, it becomes comfortable to fall into sadness and feel sorry for yourself. It can be easy to walk around with the dark cloud and not be aware of it. In the trials we face, the Lord walks with us and before us in solidarity. Scripture reminds us to have perseverance because we will grow to maturity in these seasons. Despite the difficulty, we press on with hope in Christ.

Although we can experience some joy while taking a walk through the woods or going for a road trip, delighting in creation, God's Word is clear that *pure* joy comes from the Father. Through these seasons of stress, the Lord tells us to rejoice! But how? When we are abiding with Christ and Christ in us, we have supernatural access to joy and peace through His Spirit. (See John 15:7; Acts 13:52.) It's true that we cannot manifest joy and peace on our own, especially in trials and tribulations, but we have access to a God who is mightier and greater than we are.

Here are a few ideas to stay connected to God during trials and abide in Christ:

+ Keep a prayer journal

+ Write a song or poem of thanksgiving

+ Stay faithful in your church community and time with fellow believers

+ Listen to worship music

+ Start your day with silence and Scripture

+ Take a walk and just talk to God

+ Cherish Scripture and read it every day

In a stress season, the devil wants us to feel alone, but those feelings of isolation are not from the Lord.

> *Though one may be overpowered, two can defend themselves. A cord of three strands is not quickly broken.*
> (Ecclesiastes 4:12 NIV)

Remember that people need community and connection. One of the ways we abide with Christ is by communion with His people. It can be tempting to skip church, community groups, social gatherings, prayer, or time in God's Word during a stressful season, but these are likely to be the very things that will get you through it in hope and joy. Cling to these things, for God calls them good.

SHIFT IN FOCUS

How can you get creative in spending time with the Lord?

Even if you are not in a season of stress, what part does Christian fellowship play in your life?

10 DAYS OF FUN AND JOY
Going to Seven in Growth

DAY 51 • • • • • • • • • • •
Seasons of Growth

Every good gift and every perfect gift is from above,
coming down from the Father of lights, with whom there is
no variation or shadow due to change.
(James 1:17)

As we talked about in the beginning of our conversation about
stress, thinking of your life in seasonal terms is not only biblical,
but it also gives you a lot more grace and hope for your circumstances. Seasons of stress are the opposite of seasons of growth.
The latter are periods in your life in which you feel as if you have
room to breathe, have more energy, and can focus on spiritual,
mental, and physical growth.

Seasons of growth are often blurry or over-romanticized
when we look back at our life as a whole. We either can't remember a time in our life that we didn't feel the hum of anxiety and
stress, or we can't live fully in the present because no season will
ever be as good as it has been in the past.

Both of these thought processes are unfruitful because
they're extremes. There is always a mixture of good and bad in
every situation; only the details change. This is a result of living

in a fallen world. We are living outside of our natural habitat, and it often feels like a paradox of good and bad at the same time.

Now, this doesn't mean that seasons of stress and growth coexist all the time; often, they don't. Circumstances in our lives often tip the scales. Nothing is ever all bad or all good. Working in a toxic environment or the death of a loved one will send us into a season of stress. Likewise, getting our dream job, hitting a sweet spot with parenting, or flourishing in a good friendship can tip the scale to seasons of growth.

You should push yourself during seasons of growth. Have you been wanting to read a certain book or join a Bible study? Do it! Are you thinking about starting a diet or exercising more? Now's the time! We literally have more mental space, more energy, and more bandwidth when we are in seasons of growth.

We can also see a lot of encouraging behaviors pop up. Press into them and build them in a way that they'll stick beyond this season. Create good habits that will serve a future, stressed-out you. Consistent Bible reading is a must for all of life, but especially those hard days when you feel lost.

Growth seasons are the days of digging deep and reaping the rewards. These seasons are a gift from a heavenly Father who loves you and wants to give you good things.

As we see in 1 Peter 4:10, we should be using these seasons of *good gifts* to not only build up our faith, but also to help others. In the next nine days, you'll see how going to Seven in growth helps you specifically with this, and how you can push into your growth number in a practical way.

SHIFT IN FOCUS

Are you currently in a season of growth?

Do you have a couple of good seasons in your past that you might be over-romanticizing, or maybe are ungrateful for?

● ● ● ● ● ● ● ● ● ● ● ● **DAY 52**

How Do I "Go to Seven" in Growth?

A joyful heart is good medicine.
(Proverbs 17:22)

In seasons of growth, Ones pick up the positive behaviors of an Enneagram Seven, the Enthusiast. As someone who is married to a One, I can tell you that this shift into Seven-ish behaviors is very fun to watch and brings a lot of joy to those around the One.

For example, when my husband is in seasons of growth, he laughs more, he talks more, and he's more spontaneous and very playful. These seasons are a gift because I feel like my husband is lighter and more himself. I'm not hearing his inner critic coming out as much as I normally do. His dark cloud is nowhere in sight; he's more social and motivated.

Even a random game day at work can bring out these traits in my husband, as I think we can all agree that game day is definitely a Seven's turf. My husband is someone who wears a tie every day; he is generally pretty quiet and very focused at work. But when it comes to games, he's loud, fun, expressive, and really into it. He surprises everyone but himself and those who know him well enough to see his Seven side.

Sevens are considered one of the highest energy numbers on the Enneagram, and they're all about finding the next adventure or fun thing to do or try. Sevens are easy to spot because they often embody joy and spread it like candy at a parade. We all love a healthy Seven in their element.

As a One, you are likely to recognize some of this in yourself, and it might surprise you to know that not everyone feels this lightness and joy when they are in seasons of growth. It just seems so *logical* to be more Seven-ish in growth seasons.

Not every Enneagram type needs fun, spontaneity, or laughter to be their *growth work*, but you do. In fact, most of the *work* Ones have to do in growth is letting go and having fun. This can be particularly hard; you're motivated by being *good*. It can feel like you need to be *doing good*. Fun and joy don't feel like they're accomplishing anything. You might instead feel like you're forgetting something you should be doing. It requires a lot of faith to let go and trust God that this is indeed good for you.

SHIFT IN FOCUS

Are you in a season of growth right now?

If not, when was the last time you can recognize going to Seven?

Are there certain events or situations that bring out this side of you?

• • • • • • • • • • • • **DAY 53**

The Best of Type Seven

Do not be grieved, for the joy of the Lord is your strength.
(Nehemiah 8:10)

Enneagram Sevens are spontaneous, enthusiastic, upbeat, and usually extroverted individuals. When healthy, Sevens focus their energy on their talents, goals, brightening moods, and building thriving relationships. Healthy Sevens are a bright light to an otherwise distracted and overwhelmed world. They remind us that there is always something for which to be grateful and celebrations are one of the gifts of being alive.

On the other hand, when Sevens are unhealthy, they will be scattered, irrational, and irresponsible, chasing anything that'll give them a momentary high at the cost of all else. These negative traits might make you cringe at the thought of becoming more like a Seven, but trust me, a little Seven-ness is just what your doctor ordered.

You can't truly shine without positive Seven behaviors. This is how God wired you. Sevens have something that Ones need, just like Ones have something Fours need, and so on. No one is perfect. We all have areas we need to grow in. It just so happens to be outlined really well in the system of the Enneagram what your particular personality needs to work on. We are often unaware of our own blind spots and weaknesses.

So what does going to Seven in growth look like?

+ It looks like becoming more optimistic and not only noticing the flaws in your surroundings

+ It looks like having endless good ideas for fun things to do

+ It looks like not being as critical of yourself or others

+ It looks like laughter

+ It looks like not being as fixated on making things perfect

+ It looks like enjoying planning for the future

Seven-ness equals freedom and joy in the life of a One. These are very necessary for a One's spiritual growth and sanity.

SHIFT IN FOCUS

Do you have Sevens in your life?

What do you appreciate and admire about them?

Have you ever noticed that what's hard for you seems to be very easy to them?

• • • • • • • • • • • • **DAY 54**

Growing in Joy

For freedom Christ has set us free; stand firm therefore,
and do not submit again to a yoke of slavery.
(Galatians 5:1)

What is stealing joy in your life?

As you contemplate going to Seven in growth, and the ways Sevens reflect joy, it can be frustrating not to see this growth behavior *stick* in your own life. You may experience seasons or moments of joy, but if you want joy to be more than a passing trend in your heart, you must identify the joy stealers that are getting too much of your attention.

COMPARISON

I often struggle with comparison and envy. I am quick to compare my talents to others' talents, or compare my body to someone else's. As we've all heard, "Comparison is the thief of joy"—and I, for one, can confirm that this is true. I notice myself comparing my life to others on social media and feeling bad about my life. Because of this, I purge my social media feed regularly; I unfollow accounts that cause me to fall into temptation and are not helping my overall mental state. This has helped me to stop making comparisons a habit and routine in my daily life.

ANXIETY

Anxiety and worry are other joy-stealing temptations that are easy to fall into. Anxiety is a state of perpetual worry and fixation on the things that we can't control. (We are not talking about actual mental illness here, which is different and should be treated by consulting with a professional.)

As we all struggle with control in some way or another, anxiety can be a loud symptom of our longing to be God in our own lives. However, Jesus tells us to cast our anxieties on Him and live without the burden of anxiety—not because we need to pull ourselves up by our bootstraps, but because He is in control and He goes before us, so we can trust Him in faith. (See 1 Peter 5:7; Matthew 6:25–34.)

EXPECTATIONS

Unrealistically high expectations, both for ourselves and others, can keep us in a state of perpetual frustration. Enneagram Ones are in the Idealist triad, along with Sevens and Fours, so having high expectations often comes with the territory. However, expectations for performance-based activities like special events, work, or school can contribute to anxiety and comparison. Someone might tell you that your expectations are "too high" or "unobtainable." Do these words feel like an accusation, or do you humbly reevaluate your expectations under the lens of what is practical and doable in the situation?

This list could go on and on with the things that threaten to steal our joy, but what we should learn from them all is that we are not slaves to these joy stealers. We have freedom in Christ, and acknowledging what is stealing joy from your life is the first step to living out the freedom God has already given to you in Christ.

In Galatians 5:1, Paul tells the Galatians not to submit to the yoke of slavery because we are to live out of freedom in Christ. We chose slavery when we submit to the chains of worry, guilt, comparison, high expectations, frustration, and the myriad of other joy stealers.

When we label these things in this way, they become less attractive, leading us to think of them as more of a *choice* rather than a reaction. You might be operating out of the assumption that high expectations are just part of who you are, and anxiety is just a part of life. Although there is some truth to this, you cannot take the Holy Spirit's work in your life out of the equation.

You can change; with the Holy Spirit's help, you can choose to not submit to these things.

SHIFT IN FOCUS

Name some joy stealers in your life:

1. _____

2. _____

3. _____

4. _____

5. _____

How would it change your perspective on these things to think of them in light of Galatians 5:1?

DAY 55 • • • • • • • • • • •

Growing in Spontaneity
By Lydia Sergio

You have turned for me my mourning into dancing;
you have loosed my sackcloth and clothed me with gladness.
(Psalm 30:11)

I have to push myself to be spontaneous. I'm a routine person, and I like structure. I like to know what's going to happen next and how to plan. Sometimes I get so focused on the work and tasks in front of me, I forget to laugh. I forget to relax, have fun, and *enjoy* the present moment.

I'm thankful for the close friends and family members who help me grow in this area. The other day, my sister turned on the music in our living room and started dancing. I was working on my computer and she said, "Lydia! Come join me!" I quickly replied, "No." Then she asked me to join her again. When I looked up at her, I noticed she was laughing and being silly, so I joined her! She encouraged me to jump in right alongside her spontaneous joy, and I laughed so hard! It was so good for my spirit!

Sometimes spontaneity can be uncomfortable or inconvenient. Sometimes I don't want to be spontaneous and goofy, but it's good for my soul. It's good for me to watch a comedy movie that makes me laugh, or go out for ice cream with friends on a summer night, even if it wasn't planned in advance.

Here are some ways you might practice spontaneity:

- Dance! Turn on the music and grab your kids or loved ones to join you

- The next time you go to a restaurant, order something new

- Feeling lonely? Text a friend to see if they want to go get coffee right now

- It's okay to ditch food rules every now and then. Eat cereal for dinner!

- Make sure you do something fun on one of your days off

- Try eating at a new restaurant

Sometimes what I would choose for myself is sackcloth and ashes, seriousness, and duty, but God wants to cloth me in gladness and dancing. The question is, will I let Him? Will I see spontaneous joy as a good thing, and say yes? I think we can all work on saying "yes" to God's prompting more.

SHIFT IN FOCUS

Is spontaneity easy or hard for you?

What does God's Word say about spontaneity?

Reflect on this. How will you grow in the area of spontaneity to have fun?

DAY 56 • • • • • • • • • • • •

Growing in Thankfulness
By Lydia Sergio

Mary therefore took a pound of expensive ointment made from pure nard, and anointed the feet of Jesus and wiped his feet with her hair. The house was filled with the fragrance of the perfume.
(John 12:3)

Let's chat about thankfulness. The verse above is an example of living in thankfulness. Mary's sacrifice was an act of pure, thankful worship toward Jesus. She essentially poured out gratitude onto him; she gave all that she had and held nothing back. Jesus was honored by her act of thankfulness and loved it!

In the Gospel of Luke, ten diseased men asked Jesus to heal them. Jesus had mercy on them, and they went away, but then *"one of them, when he saw that he was healed, turned back, praising God with a loud voice; and he fell on his face at Jesus' feet, giving him thanks"* (Luke 17:15–16).

I wonder what happened to the nine others who didn't express gratitude. What a greater blessing for the one who did thank Jesus!

Thankfulness is an act of worship to the Lord. A heart filled with gratitude is a joyous place to be. No matter our circumstances, we must continually live in thankfulness. My grandma is someone who offers a grateful heart continually. During my grandpa's declining health and dementia, she remained thankful.

She read her Bible and gave thanks to the Lord consistently during this time. My grandpa has passed, but she still gives thanks for their life together and their family.

> *Through him then let us continually offer up a sacrifice of praise to God, that is, the fruit of lips that acknowledge his name.*   (Hebrews 13:15)

Here are some ideas to practice thankfulness in your everyday life:

+ Keep a gratitude journal and write something in it daily

+ Tell someone what Jesus is doing in your life right now

+ Write a card or send a text to someone you care about

+ Volunteer and serve in your community or at your church

+ Don't let occasions slip by without celebrating them, no matter how small the celebration may be

SHIFT IN FOCUS

How do you practice thankfulness?

Can you see thankfulness as being good for your heart?

Who in your life do you think is gifted in thankful thinking?

DAY 57 • • • • • • • • • • • •

Growing in Hope
By Lydia Sergio

Our soul waits for the LORD; he is our help and our shield.
For our heart is glad in him, because we trust in his holy name.
(Psalm 33:20–21)

As Ones go to Seven in growth, our outlook on life becomes more positive. Our self-talk is less critical. We're hopeful as we look toward the future, and we feel excited for change.

Faith and hope work in concert together: you must have faith to have hope. And hope will give you meaning and purpose in life.

A few years ago, I experienced a major disappointment within my church leadership. I felt a loss of control; I was confused, hurt, and frustrated with choices that others made for me. I went through a season of despair and stress, but this became a time of growth for me. I chose to believe that God's plan was bigger than my plan, and I remained hopeful. I was determined to continue to live by faith. In that season, I moved from disappointment to hope and finding fresh purpose. I studied Scripture and journaled my thoughts. I verbally processed with a couple of close friends and they encouraged me.

Similarly, Hannah also experienced despair and hope because she was childless. (See 1 Samuel 1.) On a yearly trip to the temple, she prayed earnestly for God to bless her with a child. In that prayer, she made a promise to give the child back to God for His service. God blessed her with a son, whom she named Samuel. Her hope was realized and she kept her promise to God. Because of her faithfulness, God blessed her with five more children!

Here are some ideas to practice hope:

+ Speak positive verbal affirmations

+ Choose to be around friends who speak life over you

+ Journal your thoughts to help you process them

SHIFT IN FOCUS

What Scriptures do you claim as a promise of hope?

Where have you experienced moving toward hope?

DAY 58 • • • • • • • • • • • •

Growing in Vision
By Lydia Sergio

For I know the plans I have for you, declares the LORD,
plans for welfare and not for evil, to give you a future and a hope.
(Jeremiah 29:11)

Dear One, here on earth, the Lord gives each of us a vision, a purpose. Jesus declares in the Scripture above that He creates great plans for our future. He calls us uniquely to use the gifts He's blessed us with for His ministry. (See 1 Peter 4:10.) Each of us is called to a unique purpose, all to bring Him glory.

Four weeks ago, I was challenged with my lack of purpose. When I'm in a healthy space, I often have a clear vision for my future, but in this season, I didn't see the purpose clearly in front of me; I felt discouraged and lacked passion. I spent a week in constant prayer and asked the Lord to reveal His plan to me. I shared this with two people who are close to me and I asked them to pray with me.

On a Monday soon afterward, the Lord clearly renewed my purpose. He reminded me that I'm called to live a life of ministry for Jesus, whether it's working at my church, working through my business, or on my personal Instagram account. I'm called to share Jesus with the people near me. I felt peace and excitement!

God never promises that we will see the full picture of His plan for us here on earth. And as a One, I struggle with being patient in God's timing. When I feel this tension between my desire to know and my need to trust God, I've discovered it's an opportunity to not lose heart. God is faithful.

When we are in a growth season, having vision, purpose, and hope for the future becomes easier. Going to Seven—with a Seven's joy, fun, and sense of adventure—helps us with this. Normally what might seem overwhelming becomes hopeful, and it's easier to trust God with what is next. These are signs of growth in your heart.

SHIFT IN FOCUS

Have you ever prayed and asked God to give you purpose and vision?

Do you ever choose a new word for your New Year on January 1? This is one of the many ways people promote vision and purpose in their life.

Another way to enjoy a season of growth is to brainstorm a five-year plan with your spouse or loved ones and get excited about the possibilities ahead of you.

DAY 59 • • • • • • • • • • • •

Growing in Long-Suffering

We rejoice in our sufferings, knowing that suffering produces
endurance, and endurance produces character,
and character produces hope.
(Romans 5:3–4)

Long-suffering is a way that Enneagram Sevens reflect the character of God. This trait is quieter than the others they reflect, such as joy and hope, but it is altogether beautiful to observe.

Long-suffering means having or showing patience in spite of troubles, especially those caused by other people. Sevens do this by turning the other cheek, forgiving, being patient with others, offering second chances, and remaining strong when those around them fall apart.

Long-suffering is a self-sacrificing practice that doesn't give in to the emotion of the moment, but chooses grace and waits to mourn, be angry, or otherwise react.

Are you feeling a little squirmy in your seat? If so, it's okay. Long-suffering is not something that comes very naturally to Ones, but it's a huge step toward health and growth for Ones to practice.

As someone who strives for perfection, dear One, it's likely you find it hard to be patient. Your gut response to things being right or wrong doesn't leave much room for grace or a second opinion. Learning to temper these excesses of your own personality can help you become a much more long-suffering person.

But how do Ones do this? Like any fruit of the Spirit, patience is the fruit of a right relationship with God. Pure long-suffering, and the patience that comes with it, is only the hard-wrought work of the Holy Spirit within you. You can't force patience and you can't force spiritual growth or achieve it in three steps, but you can be aware of your weakness and ask your Father in heaven to help you.

> *If any of you lacks wisdom, let him ask God, who gives generously to all without reproach, and it will be given him.*
> (James 1:5)

SHIFT IN FOCUS

What is an example of long-suffering you can think of from Jesus's life on earth?

Spend some time in prayer asking God to help you grow in patience and long-suffering. If it reflects your heart, please borrow the words below:

> Dear heavenly Father, I thank You that through You, all things are possible, even making my impatient heart a patient heart through the work of Your Spirit. I thank You that You have enabled me to recognize this weakness in myself and I ask that You would help me to be continually convicted and turn to You for help. Help me to become a more long-suffering and patient One. My soul so desires this change. Amen.

DAY 60 • • • • • • • • • • • •

The Fun One

Practice these things, immerse yourself in them,
so that all may see your progress.
(1 Timothy 4:15)

At first, prioritizing growth may feel like jumping off a cliff. Every moment you are convicted to act and don't, the reality of acting becomes scarier in your head. Again and again, you may fail to take the jump because it just seems too hard. Then you'll feel beaten down and *not enough*.

This is the challenge of being a One and being motivated by goodness. You may want to grow, but you're afraid of doing so imperfectly, so you think it's not worth trying, or maybe you believe that you can't change. This feeling is something Satan uses to make sure you never walk in the freedom of your worth in Christ.

Satan is all about stopping your growth from coming to fruition. I wouldn't be surprised if you even notice elements of spiritual attack as you prioritize growth. However, that doesn't mean the growth isn't God' heart for you.

Going to Seven in growth will feel painful at times, and you'll get discouraged. Remember that life is seasonal, and you will not achieve your *ultimate* state of growth here on earth. You cannot become your ideal self because you will never be without a sin nature while you're still breathing. Yet you are still growing!

By the power of the Holy Spirit, you are in the process of becoming a beautiful person.

Don't let two steps forward and one step back discourage you. This is still moving forward; this is still growth!

Action may feel like jumping off a cliff because you're trusting God for the outcome. You're trusting that joy is better than being right. You're trusting that God is the judge, not you or anyone else. Like the child at the edge of the pool jumping into their father's arms, you're trusting that God is ready to catch you.

SHIFT IN FOCUS

Here, we are going to use this Scripture as a guideline for action:

Practice these things, immerse yourself in them, so that all may see your progress.   (1 Timothy 4:15)

"Practice these things"

You had to practice every new thing you've ever done. Growing by going to Seven is no different. Practice letting go of imperfections...plan for fun...choose one action that can be your next right thing...tell your inner critic that it's not as correct as God is and you won't listen to it. Don't be afraid to be in the mindset of spontaneity. Every small step counts.

"Immerse yourself in them"

What verse that we mentioned over the last ten days really stuck out to you? I would encourage you to memorize it, write it out, and post it somewhere you will see it. Immerse yourself in the truth of your worth in Christ, and you'll find yourself slowly but surely believing it to be true.

"So that all may see your progress"

Pick a couple of people in your life to share your big or small victories with. I hope a couple of people come to mind right away, but if they don't, there are plenty of Instagram or Facebook pages for Ones who would love to cheer you on in your One-ish wins. Be bold and share them as something worth celebrating. Go get yourself a coffee, or have a bowl of ice cream! Life is hard, and any victories are worth celebrating with God and others.

BOOK RECOMMENDATIONS
FOR ONES

Aundi Kolber, *Try Softer: A Fresh Approach to Move Us out of Anxiety, Stress, and Survival Mode—and into a Life of Connection and Joy* (Carol Stream, IL: Tyndale House Publishers, 2020)

Brené Brown, *The Gifts of Imperfection: Let Go of Who You Think You're Supposed to Be and Embrace Who You Are* (Center City, MN: Hazelden Publishing, 2010)

Dan Allender, *Leading with a Limp: Take Full Advantage of Your Most Powerful Weakness* (Colorado Springs, CO: WaterBrook Press, 2006)

Jen Wilkin, *None Like Him: 10 Ways God Is Different from Us (and Why That's a Good Thing)* (Wheaton, IL: Crossway, 2016)

Hannah Anderson, *All That's Good: Recovering the Lost Art of Discernment* (Chicago, IL: Moody Publishers, 2018)

Alison Cook and Kimberly Miller, *Boundaries for Your Soul: How to Turn Your Overwhelming Thoughts and Feelings into Your Greatest Allies* (Nashville, TN: Nelson Books, 2018)

Peter Scazzero, *Emotionally Healthy Spirituality: It's Impossible to Be Spiritually Mature, While Remaining Emotionally Immature* (Grand Rapids, MI: Zondervan, 2006)

Bob Goff, *Love Does: Discover a Secretly Incredible Life in an Ordinary World* (Nashville, TN: Thomas Nelson, 2012)

Sharon Garlough Brown, *Sensible Shoes: A Story about the Spiritual Journey* (Downers Grove, IL: InterVarsity Press, 2013)

Leeana Tankersley, *Begin Again: The Brave Practice of Releasing Hurt and Receiving Rest* (Grand Rapids, MI: Revell, 2018)

Randall Arthur, *Wisdom Hunter* (New York, NY: Multnomah, 2009)

Shauna Niequist, *Present Over Perfect: Leaving Behind Frantic for a Simpler, More Soulful Way of Living* (Grand Rapids, MI: Zondervan, 2016)

As the Enneagram has passed through many hands, and been taught by various wonderful people, I want to acknowledge that none of the concepts or ideas of the Enneagram have been created by me. I'd like to give thanks to the Enneagram teachers and pioneers who have gone before me, and whose work has influenced this devotional:

Suzanne Stabile

Ian Morgan Cron

Father Richard Rhor

Don Richard Riso

Russ Hudson

Beatrice Chestnut

Beth McCord

Ginger Lapid-Bogda

ABOUT THE AUTHOR

Elisabeth Bennett first discovered the Enneagram in the summer of 2017 and immediately realized how life-changing this tool could be. She set out to absorb all she could about this ancient personality typology, including a twelve-week Enneagram Certification course taught by Beth McCord, who has studied the Enneagram for more than twenty-five years.

Elisabeth started her own Enneagram Instagram account (@ Enneagram.Life) in 2018, which has grown to nearly 65,000 followers. Since becoming a certified Enneagram coach, Elisabeth has conducted more than one hundred one-on-one coaching sessions to help her clients find their type and apply the Enneagram to their lives for personal and spiritual growth. She has also conducted staff/team building sessions for businesses and high school students.

Elisabeth has lived in beautiful Washington State her entire life and now has the joy of raising her own children there with her husband, Peter.

To contact Elisabeth, please visit:

www.elisabethbennettenneagram.com

www.instagram.com/enneagram.life